Careers in the US Special Forces

Melissa Abramovitz

San Diego, CA

About the Author

Melissa Abramovitz is an award-winning author/freelance writer who has been writing professionally for thirty years. She specializes in writing nonfiction magazine articles and books for all age groups and has published hundreds of magazine articles, more than forty educational books for children and teenagers, numerous poems and short stories, and several children's picture books. Abramovitz graduated from the University of California, San Diego, with a degree in psychology and is also a graduate of the Institute of Children's Literature.

© 2016 ReferencePoint Press, Inc.
Printed in the United States

For more information, contact:
ReferencePoint Press, Inc.
PO Box 27779
San Diego, CA 92198
www. ReferencePointPress.com

Picture Credits

Cover: Senior Chief Petty Officer Andrew McKaskle, US Navy

7: Accurate Art, Inc
10: Tech Sgt. Joshua J. Garcia/US Army
27: © Stocktrek Images/Corbis
49: © Ed Darack/Science Faction/Corbis
56: US Air Force/Staff Sgt. Kelly Goonan

LIBRARY OF CONGRESS CATALOGING-IN-PUBLICATION DATA

Abramovitz, Melissa, 1954-
  Careers in the US Special Forces / by Melissa Abramovitz.
    pages cm. -- (Military careers)
Includes bibliographical references and index.
ISBN 978-1-60152-942-8 (hardback) -- ISBN 1-60152-942-2 (hardback) 1.
Special forces (Military science)--United States--Vocational guidance. I. Title.
  UA34.S64A28 2016
  356'.1602373--dc23
                                                    2015034205

Contents

Military Superheroes

All military personnel perform heroic deeds in defending the United States, but those in special forces, or special operations, have achieved superhero status because of their abilities and devotion to carrying out the most dangerous, secretive missions. Special forces are elite units composed of highly skilled operators with extraordinary physical, mental, and emotional strength. Whether an operator is an Army Night Stalker flying helicopters fast and low at night to sneak into enemy territory or a Navy SEAL (Sea, Air and Land teams) chasing terrorists underwater, special forces personnel regularly achieve what most people consider impossible.

The specific criteria for selecting operators vary among service branches, but all center around choosing people with moral, physical, and mental qualities that allow them to serve selflessly in dangerous circumstances. Indeed, all special operations mottoes and creeds contain similar language. For example, excerpts from the Green Beret creed state, "I am a volunteer, knowing full well the hazards of my profession. . . . I serve quietly, not seeking recognition or accolades. My goal is to succeed in my mission—and live to succeed again."

Special Forces Branches

All five military branches have their own special forces units, but all, except the Coast Guard, are under the umbrella of the Special Operations Command (SOCOM). The Coast Guard's special forces are part of the Department of Homeland Security. SOCOM unifies and coordinates these teams so they work together to address national security issues, particularly those relating to terrorism.

About sixty-six thousand people worked under SOCOM in 2015, including active duty, reserve, and support personnel in all military branches and at SOCOM headquarters. About twenty-seven thousand of these individuals work in a variety of jobs in seven units under the Army Special Operations Command. Army Green Berets, for example, specialize in forging military and political alliances in foreign countries, but they also perform reconnaissance (information gathering), raids, and counterterrorism missions. Each team member also specializes in one job as an expert in weapons, communications, engineering, or medicine, but all personnel can perform all of these jobs.

The approximately 3,000 people in the Coast Guard's Deployable Specialized Forces are on eight teams, including Port Security, which patrols, inspects boats, and enforces the law in ports and coastal areas. The Air Force Special Operations Command has about 19,500 people in its four units. One unit is Combat Control, which directs air traffic, performs reconnaissance, and protects other special operations teams. The Naval Special Warfare (NSW) Command oversees about 10,000 people in five teams that primarily conduct missions at sea. Navy SEALs, however, often perform land- and air-based missions, such as in 2011, when SEALs killed terrorist Osama bin Laden in Abbottabad, Pakistan. The 3,000 people in the Marine Corps Special Operations Command's eight teams also perform a variety of jobs on land, sea, and air. Force Recon, for example, specializes in reconnaissance, but operators also capture terrorists, raid other countries' oil and gas platforms during conflicts, and rescue hostages.

Joining the Military

The first step toward a special forces career is visiting a military recruiter, who helps an individual decide which branch of service is best for him or her. Individuals can enter the military either as an officer or as an enlisted person and can sign on for active duty (full time) or reserves (which is part time but can become full time). Officers can be commissioned or noncommissioned. Commissioned officers receive their commission after completing Reserve Officers' Training Corps (ROTC) courses at a college or university, after completing Officer Candidate School following graduation from a civilian college, or after graduating from one of the military academies, where candidates also earn a bachelor of science degree. In some cases, enlisted personnel can become commissioned officers. Other times, they can become noncommissioned officers (known as warrant or petty officers) after training in a military occupational specialty (MOS).

The MOS for which an individual is best qualified is determined by an enlisted candidate's scores on the Armed Services Vocational Aptitude Battery (ASVAB) tests given to all new recruits. Many high schools offer the ASVAB for students exploring a military career. The test asks questions in ten areas, such as general science, arithmetic reasoning, paragraph comprehension, and mechanical comprehension. Most special operations units require candidates to train in a certain MOS before applying for a special operations position. For example, army personnel who wish to be considered for the Night Stalkers must be trained in one MOS on a list of nearly fifty specialties. Examples of these specialties include avionics specialist, machinist, intelligence analyst, and electrician.

An individual's enlisted (E) or officer (O) rank, followed by a number, determines his or her uniform insignia and pay grade, which is standardized throughout the military. But different service branches have different titles for each rank. For instance, O-1, the lowest officer rank, is a second lieutenant in the Army, Marines, and Air Force and an ensign in the Navy and Coast Guard. The E-1 rank is a private in the Army and Marines, a seaman recruit in the Navy and Coast Guard, and an airman in the Air Force.

Future Outlook

Military experts believe the need for special forces officers and enlisted personnel will increase in the future as the need to fight terrorism in unconventional ways continues. But motivating people to apply for and stay in these jobs is difficult because they involve frequent and lengthy deployments. A July 2015 article in the *San Diego Union-Tribune* highlighted this issue, concluding, "U.S. special operations forces have no time to rest, let alone catch their breath." In June 2015 SOCOM commander General Joseph Votel announced plans to address this issue with new policies allowing operators more time at home.

In the US Armed Forces, pay for both enlisted personnel and officers depends on rank and years of service. Promotions depend on performance in addition to number of years served, with higher ranks translating to higher pay grades. The two graphs show monthly salaries commonly reached in the first four years of service.

Enlisted Pay

Monthly Salary Ranges for Enlisted Personnel with 0–4 Years in Service

	< 2 Years	2 Years	3 Years	4 Years

$2,580.60

Pay Grade	E-1	E-2	E-3	E-4	E-5
< 2 Years	$1,546.80	$1,734.00	$1,823.40	$2,019.60	$2,202.90
2 Years	$1,546.80	$1,734.00	$1,938.00	$2,122.80	$2,350.80
3 Years	$1,546.80	$1,734.00	$2,055.30	$2,238.00	$2,464.50
4 Years	$1,546.80	$1,734.00	$2,055.30	$2,351.40	$2,580.60

$1,546.80

Officer Pay

Monthly Salary Ranges for Officers with 0–4 Years in Service

$7,242.90

Pay Grade	O-1	O-2	O-3	O-4	O-5	O-6
< 2 Years	$2,934.30	$3,380.70	$3,912.60	$4,449.90	$5,157.60	$6,186.60
2 Years	$3,054.30	$3,850.20	$4,435.20	$5,151.30	$5,810.10	$6,796.80
3 Years	$3,692.10	$4,434.30	$4,787.10	$5,495.10	$6,212.10	$7,242.90
4 Years	$3,692.10	$4,584.00	$5,219.40	$5,571.60	$6,288.00	$7,242.90

$2,934.30

Note: Monthly salary ranges in both graphs are based on enlisted and officer pay scales effective January 1, 2015. The pay scales described here do not take into account the value of health benefits or housing and other allowances.

Source: Defense Finance and Accounting Service, "Military Pay Charts, 1949 to 2015," December 23, 2014. www.dfas.mil/militarymembers/payentitlements/military-pay-charts.html.

Another issue concerning special operations is the inclusion of female special operators. By January 2016 all units are to begin admitting women or to explain why this is not possible. Surveys taken after this order was issued indicated that many men in these formerly all-male teams opposed it. Many believed the stringent physical fitness standards would be lowered to allow women to succeed, despite Votel's promise to the contrary. In August 2015, after First Lieutenant Shaye Haver and Captain Kristen Greist became the first females to graduate from the grueling Army Ranger School (required for all candidates for the Army's special operations Ranger team), the debate on this issue intensified. Although Haver and Greist fulfilled the same requirements as the male graduates, women who have tried to pass Marine Corps infantry training and similar programs have not achieved adequate physical fitness scores. The military thus continued to debate whether females were fit to serve in formerly all-male combat units. Although Haver and Greist earned their Ranger tabs, they will not be eligible to serve in a Ranger unit until the Army opens the Rangers to all graduates.

Another widespread concern is that women might disrupt team unity and mission success by causing sexual distractions. One former Ranger told NBC News, "Throwing a woman in the middle of a team like that is just going to make the entire team useless because in the end, there will be so much infighting, so much drama" over sexual attraction. Yet in the same news article, Marine Corps captain Colleen Farrell, who served with other women in noncombat roles in Afghanistan, disagreed: "When you have elite teams where the level of discipline is just so high, I really don't think that's going to be a problem. Those Special Operations soldiers and Marines who are over there, they are there for the mission. They're not in Afghanistan to get married." This issue, which parallels controversies over combat roles for women in the rest of the military, will probably remain controversial as special forces evolve in the future.

Army Green Berets

What Does a Green Beret Do?

At a Glance:
Army Green Berets

Minimum Educational Requirements
Enlisted: high school diploma or GED; officers: bachelor's degree

Personal Qualities
Intelligent, self-disciplined, honorable, resilient, adaptable, physically fit

Certification
Enlisted: Army Special Forces engineering, weapons, medical, or communications sergeant certification; officers: Army Special Forces officer certification

Working Conditions
Any environment: deserts, mountains, jungles, cities

Salary Range
Monthly salary depends on pay grade and years of service

Number of Jobs
Approximately 7,000 Green Berets in 2015

Future Job Outlook
3,000 new enlisted and 400 new officers sought by Green Berets in 2015; similar needs expected next few years

The motto of Army Green Berets, also called Army Special Forces, is *De oppresso liber*—"To free the oppressed." In line with this motto, the approximately seven thousand Green Berets specialize in unconventional (guerrilla) warfare, foreign internal defense (teaching foreign armies to defend their countries), special reconnaissance (covertly gathering intelligence), direct action (striking at enemies), counterterrorism, and counterinsurgency (fighting against forces trying to overturn friendly governments). Green Berets also participate in humanitarian missions to help civilians affected by natural disasters or war. For example, in April 2015 Green Berets headed to Nepal to help with search and rescue, treating wounded people, and building shelters for homeless people after a devastating earthquake.

The Green Berets' primary role is fighting terrorist and other threats, such as drug trafficking, worldwide. Sometimes

US Army Green Berets from the Seventh Special Forces Group jump out of a C-130H3 Hercules during a 2015 special operations forces exercise in Florida. The Green Berets fight terrorist and other threats worldwide.

they prevent or respond directly to terrorist activities with lightning-fast strikes; other times they practice diplomacy to gain local support for US missions or to advise foreign leaders on best tactics. Indeed, Green Berets are often referred to as *underground diplomats* because of the many secret missions in which they negotiate with world leaders. They also train or help other countries' military forces or guerrilla fighters whose goals parallel those of America. Forging these alliances often involves adapting to the customs and practices of native populations. For example, a Green Beret team was assigned to collaborate with Afghan fighters who were battling the Islamic fundamentalist Taliban in 2001. Because these fighters rode on horses, they insisted the Americans do the same. Only one member of the Green Beret team had any horseback-riding experience, however, and the wooden Afghan saddles were extremely uncomfortable for the Americans. To remedy the situation, the Green Berets called in an urgent request for American-style saddles. Support teams air-dropped the saddles to help the team cement the alliance.

To accomplish these varied missions, the twelve men in each Green Beret team are all well versed in weapons, engineering, communications, emergency medical care, and mission planning. Nonetheless, each team member has a specialty. The team leader is an officer who is responsible for mission planning, obtaining needed supplies, and ensuring all team members are ready. Weapons specialists are experts in using, maintaining, and teaching their teams to use and defend themselves against a variety of weapons. Engineering specialists are experts in navigation; land surveying; vehicle repair; building bridges, houses, and other things the team may need; and demolitions (destroying enemy buildings, airfields, vehicles, power plants, and other assets). Communications sergeants can operate and fix every known type of communications gear, including encrypted satellite communications systems, radios, and computers. They are also responsible for communicating intelligence information to SOCOM and handling psychological operations (PSYOPS). According to SOCOM, PSYOPS seek to win the hearts and minds of native populations that US troops are trying to help, and may also include false information campaigns to confuse enemy forces. Medical sergeants are trained in emergency medicine, dentistry, optometry, veterinary care, public sanitation, and water quality, so they can assist and treat native populations as well as their own team members. According to Army Special Operations Command, Green Beret medical sergeants "are considered to be the finest first-response/trauma medical technicians in the world."

How Do You Become a Green Beret?

Schooling, Group Activities, and Volunteer Work

Because Green Berets often work in other countries and frequently interact closely with native populations, students interested in this type of career would benefit from foreign language, geography, political science, world or religious studies, and history classes that can help them understand past and present wars and conflicts. Participation in ROTC to gain an understanding of how the military operates and trains its people can also be valuable. Because physical fitness and teamwork are essential for Green Berets, students can also benefit from participation in team sports. In fact, the military states that many Army Special Forces members participated in sports like lacrosse, water polo, swimming, track, football, and wrestling in school. Participating in organizations such as Boy Scouts, which teach self-reliance, wilderness survival, and team-building skills, can also be helpful. Volunteer work in wilderness areas, with immigrant populations, or in any capacity that develops organizational skills and requires interaction with people may also be beneficial.

Skills and Personality

Individuals with the best chances of being selected for Green Berets demonstrate intelligence, integrity, self-confidence, humility, discipline, perseverance, and physical fitness. The ability to perform well under pressure, make quick decisions, and handle multiple responsibilities is also essential. Candidates who speak one or more foreign languages may also improve their chances of being accepted as Green Berets.

Qualifications

To be considered for the Green Berets, applicants must volunteer for the job and be males between the ages of twenty and thirty who are currently on active duty. In addition, volunteers for the job are required to be American citizens, eligible for a secret clearance, have vision that is correctable to 20/20, and must pass vocational, psychological, medical, and physical fitness tests. For instance, candidates must be able to swim 164 feet (50 m) while wearing boots and battle dress uniform.

Enlisted applicants must have at least a high school diploma or a general equivalency diploma (GED), must be in E-4 to E-7 pay grades, and must have at least twenty-four months of active duty remaining after qualifying for Army Special Forces. Enlisted men also must score at least 110 in the general technical category on the AS-VAB.

Officer applicants must have at least a bachelor's degree, be in O-1 or O-2 pay grades, and have at least thirty-six months of active duty remaining after qualifying for Army Special Forces. They must have at least a secret clearance and be eligible for a top secret clearance, must have completed the Officer Basic Course and have been successful in leadership assignments, and must qualify on the Defense Language Aptitude Battery or the Defense Language Proficiency Test.

Army Training and Education

All applicants undergo a grueling selection and training process. Training for enlisted men begins with a fourteen-week course that combines Basic Combat Training and Advanced Individual Training. On its website, the Army calls Basic Combat Training "the ten-week journey from civilian to soldier." Recruits learn about army customs, tactical and survival skills, and how to march, handle weapons, and rappel. Advanced Individual Training provides instruction and hands-on experience in an individual's MOS. After this, candidates attend Army Airborne Training.

The next step for enlisted men and the first for officers is to attend a special operations preparation and selection program. Candidates are subjected to many types of physical and mental stressors, including day and night marches in all types of weather while carrying 50-pound (23 kg) rucksacks, sleep deprivation, running until told to stop, obstacle courses, and being stranded with only a map and compass to navigate. Fewer than half of the original candidates go on to the next phase.

Those who pass proceed to the six-phase Special Forces Qualification Course (Q Course). Over the course of sixty to one hundred weeks, depending on MOS, candidates learn about Army Special Forces culture, history, and missions. They also receive advanced training in land navigation, marksmanship, combat, infiltration and exfiltration techniques (sneaking into and out of enemy-held areas by parachuting, land, or sea), and survival-evasion-resistance-and-escape (SERE) training. SERE teaches soldiers how to survive in any weather or environment if stranded and includes skills to avoid or deal with being captured by enemy forces. Candidates also study the language and culture of the area to which they will be sent.

Those who pass Q Course receive group assignments, academic awards, and the hallmark green beret and uniform tab after graduation. Officers become credentialed Army Special Forces officers, and enlisted graduates earn credentials as Army Special Forces weapons, engineering, communications, or medical sergeants. Medical sergeants also receive certifications as emergency medical technicians (EMTs) after passing the Special Operations Combat Medic Course. After Green Berets are assigned to a team, they continue training to maintain and improve their skills and to acquire new specialized skills.

On the Job

Working Conditions

Missions may take place in any environment, including deserts, jungles, mountains, or cities, and they may last for weeks or months. While deployed, Green Berets might live in tents without electricity and plumbing in a wilderness area. Sometimes they move from place to place using military vehicles. Other times, they ride on pack animals such as donkeys or horses. In such instances, setting up camp might involve building temporary stables for the animals. In other situations, they might stay in military barracks on a military base run by US or allied forces. Often, when their job requires them to blend in with natives, Green Berets dress like locals and live among them in apartments or houses.

While on the job, teams may be faced with a variety of climates and natural and human-made hazards, such as poisonous snakes, treacherous sandstorms, roadside bombs planted by enemy forces, and chemical and biological weapons. For example, a team that infiltrated Afghanistan in 2001 had to quickly acclimate to breathing at altitudes up to 16,000 feet (4,877 m) and to melting the ice off the helicopter rotors before their aircraft could take off again. Other missions can take place in the blistering heat of deserts, as when Green Berets deployed to Iraq during the 1990s and early 2000s faced temperatures of 110° to 120°F (43° to 49°C) and had to drink large amounts of water to prevent heatstroke.

Green Berets must also be ready for the varied responses of the locals to their presence. In Ad Diwaniyah, Iraq, in 2003, Green Berets restored electricity, set up a new police force, and reopened schools and hospitals after a battle knocked out electricity and forced schools, police, and other public services to close. In this instance, the local population was grateful for their efforts. Yet this is not always the case. In 2003 a Green Beret unit was ambushed near Ar Rutbah, Iraq, after their presence was reported to enemy troops by members of a local tribe.

Earnings

Monthly salary depends on pay grade and years of service. While deployed, Army Special Forces operators can also receive special hazard pay. Every month, operators can earn up to an extra $1,000 in language pay for speaking foreign languages, $150 in parachuting pay, $220 in dive pay, and $375 in special duty pay, though there are limits on the number of special pays. Green Berets can also receive reenlistment bonuses and are eligible for education benefits with less time served than other military specialties.

Opportunities for Advancement

Operators regularly advance in rank on the basis of achievements and time served. Because of their vast experience, many go on to screen and teach new Army Special Forces recruits as well as serving on missions. Many also advance to high-ranking military positions. For instance, Brigadier General Gary Harrell, who became commander of SOCOM in 2002, previously served with two Green Beret groups and with the Army's Delta Force.

What Is the Future Outlook for Green Berets?

In February 2015 the Army announced that it needed about three thousand new enlisted and four hundred new officers in the Green Berets. Recruiting commander Major Jason Hetzel told the *Army Times*, "With the downsizing of the Army [as the war in Afghanistan ends], the relevance of special operations has never been greater." This need should continue for at least several years.

What Are Employment Prospects in the Civilian World?

The personal qualities and experience of Green Berets make them strong candidates for many types of civilian employment after they leave the military. For example, former Green Beret Scotty Neil states in a Business Insider online article that Green Berets' self-reliance, adaptability, and experience in planning and executing complex operations make them well suited for business careers. Neil founded the Green Beret Foundation to help former Green Berets find business-related jobs or start their own businesses. The Partnership for Youth Success (PaYS) program also helps former Green Berets find jobs. This program guarantees a job interview with employers who are looking for experienced veterans; some of the companies include AT&T, Hewlett-Packard, Kraft Foods, Sears Holdings Corporation, and Walgreens. Many other former Green Berets serve in government departments as civilians, and many Green Beret medical sergeants find jobs as civilian EMTs or paramedics.

Army Night Stalkers

At a Glance:

Army Night Stalkers

Minimum Educational Requirements
Enlisted: high school diploma or GED; officers: bachelor's degree

Personal Qualities
Reliable, intelligent, trustworthy, loyal, responsible, emotionally stable, self-motivated, self-disciplined, adaptable, physically fit

Certification and Licensing
Basic mission-qualified Night Stalker after completing Basic Night Stalker Course; fully mission-qualified Night Stalker after on-the-job assessments

Working Conditions
Flying helicopters to destinations in mountains, deserts, jungles, urban settings, battlefields

Salary Range
Monthly salary depends on pay grade and years of service

Number of Jobs
About 3,000 in 2015

Future Job Outlook
Continuing need in the future

The Night Stalkers, also called the 160th Special Operations Aviation Regiment (SOAR), was organized after US special forces failed in an attempt to rescue fifty-two American diplomats held hostage at the US embassy in Iran in April 1980. Eight operators died, mostly because teams from different military branches did not coordinate their actions and because of a lack of well-trained army helicopter pilots who could fly at low levels in darkness. The latter deficiency led the Department of Defense to organize SOAR, which became known as the Night Stalkers because of its operators' expertise in flying blacked-out helicopters at night while wearing night vision and infrared goggles. Night Stalkers, who numbered about three thousand in 2015, are also known for flying at high speeds and low altitudes to avoid radar detectors. They usually conduct missions that involve inserting and extracting special operations teams on critical reconnaissance, attack, and search-and-rescue missions. They regularly train with other US special operations teams and with teams from allied nations.

Night Stalkers have transported special operations teams on many high-profile missions, such as the 2011 mission in which Navy SEALs killed terrorist Osama bin Laden in Abbottabad, Pakistan. They also transported operators to Saddam Hussein Hospital in Nasiriya, Iraq, in 2003 to rescue Private First Class Jessica Lynch, who was held hostage after she was wounded in an ambush. Lynch's rescue represented the first successful rescue of an American prisoner of war in an enemy country since World War II.

Besides flying and acting as crew members aboard army helicopters, some Night Stalkers repair these aircraft and serve in various administrative and other support positions.

How Do You Become a Night Stalker?

Schooling, Group Activities, and Volunteer Work

Because Night Stalkers can be sent anywhere in the world, students interested in this type of career would benefit from foreign language, geography, political science, world or religious studies, and history classes that help them understand past and present wars and conflicts. Flying aircraft also requires much expertise in mechanics, computer technologies, meteorology (weather and wind), and other factors that affect aircraft; therefore, classes in physics, earth science, and engineering can also be helpful. Participation in ROTC to gain an understanding of how the military operates and trains its people might also be valuable. Organizations such as Boy Scouts, which teach self-reliance, wilderness survival, first aid, and team-building skills, can also be helpful. Volunteer work in wilderness areas, in facilities that administer medical treatment, or in any capacity that develops organizational skills and requires interaction with people may also be beneficial.

Because physical fitness is heavily emphasized in selecting and training Night Stalkers, army trainers recommend staying physically fit and gradually working up to achieving the required standards. Participation in team sports such as football, lacrosse, wrestling, swimming, water polo, and track is especially good preparation for the physical fitness challenges Night Stalker candidates and operators encounter and also helps develop the robust team spirit that characterizes and drives Night Stalker teams.

Skills and Personality

The SOAR application asks questions that assess applicants' reliability, trustworthiness, loyalty, responsibility, perseverance, intelligence, physical fitness, commitment to keep all missions secret, and emotional stability, as these qualities are essential for Night Stalkers.

Qualifications

Both officers and enlisted personnel can apply to become Night Stalkers. Officers must volunteer for the job, but enlisted personnel can be assigned by army command. SOAR is one of the few special forces units to accept female candidates. Women started flying attack helicopters for the Army during the 1990s, and in 2013 they were allowed to apply for positions as Night Stalker pilots and crew chiefs. By 2015 three women had completed training as Night Stalker pilots.

All Night Stalker candidates must be on active duty, US citizens, eligible for a secret clearance, have at least three years of service remaining on their army contract, and agree to extend this contract. Officer candidates must have at least a bachelor's degree, and enlisted applicants must be high school graduates and have an MOS in a category on a specified list. Examples of these specialties include avionic mechanic, aviation specialist, electronic warfare specialist, and intelligence analyst. Enlisted candidates must also score at least 100 on the general technical category of the ASVAB.

All candidates must also be financially stable; have no drug offenses, felonies, or court martials on their record; and must agree to allow the selection committee to investigate their social media accounts. Candidates must also meet army standards for weight and physical fitness and must pass a flight physical exam, which can exclude an individual with any of a variety of medical conditions from flying an aircraft.

Army Training and Education

All Night Stalker candidates undergo extensive training in the Green Platoon Course. The officers' Green Platoon Course lasts twenty to twenty-eight weeks, and the one for enlisted personnel lasts five weeks. Candidates receive classroom instruction and hands-on training in land navigation, first-responder skills for saving lives, weapons, combat skills, and teamwork. There is also extensive practice in survival-evasion-resistance-escape (SERE) skills to teach candidates how to survive in any weather or environment if stranded. SERE also teaches skills to avoid or deal with being captured by enemy forces since special forces operators are at high risk for capture.

Since much of the work Night Stalkers do occurs at night, the Green Platoon Course involves extensive training with night vision and infrared goggles. A great deal of time is also devoted to physical fitness training and challenges, such as 4- to 6-mile (6- to 10-km) runs, 4- to 10-mile (6- to 16-km) road marches carrying 45-pound (20 kg) rucksacks, rope climbing, and calisthenics. Psychological testing and observation are also important parts of the training program. Instructors note how well candidates work with others, and psychologists conduct many interviews with students to assess their mental and emotional stability.

The most dreaded and challenging part of the Green Platoon Course is the notorious Black Day. As a test of the SOAR creed—Night Stalkers Don't Quit!—on Black Day candidates are pushed to their physical and mental limits to see who will or will not quit. These challenges, which include using teamwork to free one's team from a simulated aircraft crash in water, are designed to prepare candidates to encounter and overcome any type of situation that may arise on a mission. When asked what motivates candidates to push themselves beyond what they believe they can achieve, one soldier who successfully completed the Green Platoon Course told the *Fort Campbell Courier*, "The sense of accomplishment makes it all worthwhile."

After completing the Green Platoon Course, Night Stalkers are considered to be basic mission qualified and earn the privilege of wearing the maroon beret with the SOAR crest. Once Night Stalkers pass various other tests and achieve leadership qualifications through on-the-job experience, they are designated as fully mission qualified.

On the Job

Working Conditions

Night Stalker missions can take place anywhere in the world. When personnel are deployed, they generally live on military bases in a specific geographic region where they may be called on to fly missions. In recent years these places have included Afghanistan, Iraq, and various countries in Africa. Some missions are over quickly; for example, rescuing Jessica Lynch in Iraq took only twenty-five minutes once the teams were on the ground. Others may involve many hours of flying to a destination and remaining airborne for many hours to perform reconnaissance and protect troops on the ground. This type of mission requires a refueling aircraft to refuel the helicopters in the air. Either way, Night Stalker aircraft are often fired upon with guns, rocket-propelled grenades, and missiles, making the job extremely dangerous. In 2005, for example, during a Night Stalker mission in Afghanistan to rescue a Navy SEAL, the MH-47 Chinook helicopter was hit by a rocket-propelled grenade, killing eight Night Stalkers and eight SEALs.

Since Night Stalkers participate in the most dangerous and critical missions, the aircraft they fly are specially modified versions of army helicopters, such as the MH-60 Blackhawk, the MH-47 Chinook, and the MH-6 and AH-6 versions of the Little Bird. The aircraft are modified to allow pilots to fly in dangerous, low-visibility conditions and to allow gunner crews to defend passengers, other aircraft, and ground troops. For instance, the MH-60L Direct Action Penetrators that Night Stalkers fly contain more weapons than most MH-60s, including numerous guns, rocket pods, cannon, and missiles. All of the helicopters that Night Stalkers have flown in Afghanistan since 2001 also contain multimode radar. This technology allows pilots to see outlines of mountains and other geographic features during the adverse weather conditions and sandstorms that frequently occur in this area. As the book *Night Stalkers*, by Fred J. Pushies, explains, "Only the skilled pilots and state-of-the-art aircraft of the 160th are trained and equipped to operate in zero/zero conditions: zero visibility and zero ceiling." The fact that many mountains in Afghanistan are over

10,000 feet (3,048 m) tall means pilots must fly their aircraft higher than most helicopters fly, raising the height "ceiling" and requiring pilots and passengers to use oxygen masks to breathe.

The two special stealth Blackhawks in which Night Stalkers flew the SEAL team that killed Osama bin Laden were modified with a special shape and type of coating so they could not be detected by enemy radar. They were also much quieter than normal Blackhawks because they had extra blades on the tail rotor. One of these helicopters crashed into a wall around the target house because of wind conditions, but the pilot's exemplary skill in keeping it from tumbling when it crashed saved the team.

Earnings

Monthly salary depends on pay grade and years of service. Night Stalkers are also eligible for special hazard duty pay ranging from $150 to $240 per month and flight crew pay of $150 to $400 per month. After flying for several years, enlisted Night Stalkers can also receive flight and reenlistment bonuses that depend on rank. Officers can receive $125 to $840 per month in special aviation pay and can receive bonuses for remaining on active duty after their initial contracts end.

Opportunities for Advancement

Besides advancing in rank based on time served, Night Stalkers can be placed in positions with increasing responsibilities on the basis of tests and evaluations of their leadership qualifications after they become basic mission qualified. Once they are fully mission qualified, they can be assessed as potential crew chiefs and flight leaders after serving three to five years. There are also opportunities for Night Stalkers to become involved in selecting and training candidates who apply for the unit, and many operators go on to serve in other administrative and leadership positions in the military.

What Is the Future Outlook for Night Stalkers?

In February 2015 the Army announced it was looking for an unspecified number of new Night Stalker recruits, both male and female, to serve in the air as pilots and crew members, on the ground in helicopter maintenance and repair, and on aircraft and reconnaissance support teams. The need for new Night Stalkers should continue into the foreseeable future as special operations missions remain critical elements of military strategies around the world.

What Are Employment Prospects in the Civilian World?

The piloting, combat, first-aid, and survival skills that Night Stalkers have make them excellent candidates for jobs as helicopter pilots for search-and-rescue teams, medical evacuation, firefighting, and law enforcement in the civilian world. Their expertise in repairing and servicing aircraft also opens up civilian job opportunities. Many former Night Stalkers also go on to business careers because of their leadership and organizational skills.

Navy SEALs

At a Glance:
Navy SEALs

Minimum Educational Requirements
Enlisted: high school diploma or GED; officers: bachelor's degree

Personal Qualities
Mature, resilient, intelligent, self-motivated, eager to take on challenges, confident yet modest, trustworthy, good team player, dedicated to serving one's country, adaptable, self-disciplined, physically fit

Certification and Licensing
Combat medic, sniper, parachute jumpmaster, advanced marksman, diving supervisor, intelligence specialist certifications

Working Conditions
Oceans, rivers, mountains, jungles, deserts, urban areas

Salary Range
Monthly salary depends on pay grade and years of service

Number of Jobs
About 2,450 active duty and 600 reserve SEALs in 2015

Future Job Outlook
Continuing need for SEALs

SEALs are part of the best-known Naval Special Warfare (NSW) division. The acronym *SEAL* stands for Sea, Air and Land. The SEALs grew out of the Navy's underwater demolition teams formed during World War II. These teams cleared underwater mines. During the Vietnam War, the role of the SEALs expanded to include beach and coastal reconnaissance (intelligence gathering) along Vietnamese rivers. Today SEALs perform missions that include land warfare, counterterrorism, foreign internal defense (training and helping foreign military forces defeat insurgents and terrorists), reconnaissance, and unconventional (guerrilla) warfare. SEALs also perform many missions at sea. For instance, after Somali pirates kidnapped the captain of the commercial ship *Maersk Alabama* off the coast of Somalia in 2009, three SEAL snipers aboard the navy destroyer *Bainbridge* killed the pirates, who were pointing

AK-47 assault weapons at the hostage's head. Other SEALs quickly arrived in inflatable boats to rescue the captain.

There are nine main SEAL teams plus the highly secretive team that killed terrorist Osama bin Laden in 2011. That team, which is so secretive that it is not listed on SEAL organization charts, specializes in counterterrorism and hostage rescue missions, such as the multiagency rescue of Private Jessica Lynch in 2003 after Iraqi forces captured her during an ambush. The book *The US Special Forces: What Everyone Needs to Know*, by John Prados, calls this team "an elite within an elite."

All SEAL teams operate in sixteen-man operational task units that are assigned to specific missions. These task units often split into smaller units for specific missions. For instance, when SEALs swim or dive, they operate in two-man teams to assist and protect each other. Each SEAL on the sixteen-man teams specializes in medicine, communications, weapons, or reconnaissance, along with being cross trained to excel in all of these fields.

How Do You Become a SEAL?

Schooling, Group Activities, and Volunteer Work

Navy personnel who screen SEAL applicants stress that high academic and sports achievements in high school vastly increase the chances of being selected. Thus, taking rigorous college-prep classes in high school in all subjects, including math, science, English, and history, is encouraged. Since SEALs are sent throughout the world, classes in foreign languages, geography, political science, and world cultures are also valuable. Participation in team sports such as water polo, rugby, lacrosse, wrestling, and swimming increases the chance of being selected and succeeding as a SEAL, as does a two- or four-year college degree. Indeed, those with a degree are nearly twice as likely to become SEALs as those without a degree.

Participation in ROTC to gain an understanding of how the military operates and trains its people can also be valuable. Organizations such as Boy Scouts, which teach self-reliance, wilderness survival, and team-building skills, can also be helpful. Volunteer work in wilderness areas, with immigrant populations, or in any capacity that develops organizational skills and requires interaction with people may also be beneficial.

Skills and Personality

SEAL applicants must be dedicated to serving their country, physically fit, mentally sharp, resilient, mature, self-motivated, trustworthy, self-confident yet modest, and eager to take on challenges.

Qualifications

The SEAL program accepts applications from enlisted personnel who are new to the Navy or are already in the Navy assigned to another unit. Personnel in another service branch may apply to be a SEAL by notifying their existing commander and the NSW Command. Enlisted candidates must achieve certain minimum scores in areas such as mechanical comprehension, electronics information, and general science on the ASVAB to be considered for the program.

Candidates must then pass the Computerized Special Operations Resilience Test, which assesses mental and emotional strength and resilience, and the Physical Screening Test (PST), which includes swimming 500 yards (457 m); doing push-ups, pull-ups, and curl-ups; and running 1.5 miles (2.4 km). Those who achieve a minimum passing score can begin training with an NSW mentor, but they cannot earn a SEAL contract until their score improves. Those with an optimum PST score are more likely to be given a SEAL contract right away.

After passing the PST and several other physical and mental fitness tests, the candidate can submit a SEAL application to his navy career counselor. If selected, he will receive orders to attend the NSW Preparatory course.

Officers who wish to become SEALs begin by taking the PST. Those who achieve an optimum score then attend the SEAL Officer Assessment and Selection program, which involves high-stress physical, mental, psychological, and behavioral evaluations for two weeks. Candidates' leadership abilities and language and cultural skills are also assessed. NSW Command usually selects seventy to ninety officers to undergo SEAL officer training each year.

US Navy SEALs prepare to board a yacht in the Gulf of Mexico off of Key West, Florida. SEALs perform missions on land and at sea; they are involved in counterterrorism, in training foreign military forces, and in guerrilla warfare.

All SEAL candidates must be US citizens, obtain a secret clearance, have vision that is correctable to 20/25, and may not be color blind. Candidates must not have been convicted of any felonies involving drugs, weapons, violence, or sex, and they must be seventeen to twenty-eight years old (though highly qualified applicants aged twenty-nine or thirty may receive a waiver). The official NSW website states that SEALs must also commit to remaining "morally, mentally and physically qualified."

Navy Training and Education

Qualified enlisted and officer SEAL candidates begin the rigorous yearlong training program known as Basic Underwater Demolition/ SEAL (BUD/S) training, which starts with the NSW Preparatory course that enhances their physical fitness. The preparatory course ends with a modified PST that includes challenges such as completing a 1,000-yard (914 m) swim with fins in twenty minutes or less and doing at least seventy push-ups in under two minutes. Those who fail are dropped from training.

Those who pass go on to the NSW Orientation, where candidates are further assessed for desirable characteristics and learn about the special operations lifestyle. Of the next training stages, the most challenging is known as Hell Week. Over the course of five and a half days, candidates sleep a total of about four hours, run more than 200 miles (322 km), and complete other challenges. The NSW website states that those who complete Hell Week are the ones "who have made a full commitment to their goal of becoming a SEAL and who decide ahead of time that quitting is not an option."

The rest of SEAL training includes combat training and advanced diving skills, land warfare, medical skills, marksmanship, parachuting, demolitions, rapelling, and small-unit teamwork. Students also attend survival-evasion-resistance-escape (SERE) training to learn how to survive in any weather or environment if stranded. SERE also teaches skills to avoid or deal with being captured by enemy forces.

Only 20 to 25 percent of the individuals who start SEAL training end up graduating. Graduates are awarded the SEAL trident insignia and are then assigned to a team. They can also receive certifications as combat medics, snipers, advanced marksmen, parachute jumpmasters, diving supervisors, and intelligence specialists. Graduates then undergo another eighteen months of predeployment specialized training in medicine, weapons, communications, intelligence, or engineering. SEALs continue to train throughout their careers to maintain the skills they have mastered.

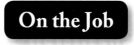

On the Job

Working Conditions

SEALs are often deployed for six to eight months per year and operate in any and all environments, including cities, mountains, deserts, jungles, and oceans. They may live in tents or other structures without electricity or running water, and may be exposed to natural and human-made hazards such as sandstorms, blizzards, poisonous snakes, explosive devices, chemical and biological weapons, and gunfire. Sometimes they live in military base barracks or housing; other times they live on ships or in cities or towns among native populations.

SEALs may arrive at their destinations by sea, land, or air, and all are qualified swimmers, divers, and parachutists. They often travel to and from their missions in NSW rigid-hull inflatable boats or in MK-V boats operated by special warfare combatant-craft crewmen. Sometimes they must swim or scuba dive part of the way. A specialized SEAL Delivery Vehicle Team travels to its missions in minisubmarines. These submarines are used for missions involving the placement of explosives on targeted ships or those involving underwater reconnaissance. Other times, SEALs may parachute or quickly descend on a rope (or, fast-rope) from aircraft, walk, travel in land vehicles, or ride pack animals such as mules.

Each mission is planned and rehearsed down to the last detail, including carefully timing swim distances to be sure the scuba tanks will have enough air. Water conditions, including temperature, currents, and possible pollutants, must also be considered to determine whether divers or swimmers will have to be decontaminated. Other factors, such as determining where to hide scuba equipment while conducting a mission, must also be planned. Officers are in charge of planning, but all team members participate.

Oftentimes things do not go as planned, so operators are always prepared to adapt. For example, in the 2011 mission in which SEALs killed Osama bin Laden, the team had to quickly change its plans after one of the helicopters used for transport crashed into a wall surrounding the house in which Bin Laden was hiding. Rather than fast-roping onto the roof as planned, the SEALs in the other helicopter landed on the ground and approached the house on that level. In another situation, high up in the mountains in Afghanistan during the winter of 2003, the rifles that the SEALs carried froze as they tried to attack enemy forces. The team had to call in aircraft to bomb the enemy. Whatever their mission may be, SEALs are known for doing whatever it takes to get the job done. As the SEAL ethos reminds each operator, wearing the SEAL trident is "a privilege that I must earn every day."

Earnings

Monthly salary depends on pay grade and years of service. In addition to their regular salary, SEALs can earn bonuses when they qualify as SEALs as well as reenlistment bonuses. They may also earn extra pay for hazardous duty assignments of $450 per month for enlisted personnel and $110 or more per month for officers. All SEALs may also earn extra monthly pay for demolitions ($150), diving ($215 to $340), parachuting ($150 to $225), and speaking a foreign language ($50 to $100), though there are limits on the number of special pays.

Opportunities for Advancement

SEAL officers generally lead a SEAL platoon for about five years and are then promoted to oversee the planning and execution of a wider range of naval and/or other military operations. Some officers go on to lead an entire naval department or to become a lead SEAL training officer. Others may be stationed overseas to work with the special operations units of allied nations or at SOCOM to coordinate planning and missions with other US special operations units.

Enlisted SEALs can be promoted faster than normal as they reach milestones in SEAL training and on-the-job missions. Many go on to train new SEALs and to enter important administrative and leadership positions in the Navy or other military commands.

What Is the Future Outlook for SEALs?

The need for new SEALs should continue into the foreseeable future as special operations missions remain critical elements of military strategies around the world.

What Are Employment Prospects in the Civilian World?

The skills that SEALs possess qualify them for jobs in many civilian areas. Many become fitness trainers or teachers or join search-and-rescue teams, medical teams, or law enforcement organizations. Others start or work for businesses or in finance-related or investment careers. The SEAL Future Fund is one organization that helps former SEALs obtain scholarships to go back to school and provides job placement assistance with a variety of companies that seek intelligent, hardworking, well-organized employees.

Navy Special Warfare Boat Operators

At a Glance:
Navy Special Warfare Boat Operators

Minimum Educational Requirements
High school diploma or GED

Personal Qualities
Dedicated to serving one's country, self-motivated, good team player, resilient, honorable, courageous, intelligent, adaptable, self-disciplined, physically fit

Certification and Licensing
special warfare combatant-craft crewmen qualified; combat medic qualified after completing the Special Operations Combat Medic Course

Working Conditions
Oceans, rivers, jungles, deserts, arctic areas

Salary Range
Monthly salary depends on pay grade and years of service

Number of Jobs
Around 750 active duty operators and 50 reserve operators in 2015

Future Job Outlook
Continuing need for operators

What Does a Navy Special Warfare Boat Operator Do?

NSW boat operators, often referred to as special warfare combatant-craft crewmen (SW-CC), originated with the so-called Brown Water Navy established in 1965 to support Navy SEALs during the Vietnam War. The Brown Water Navy operated small gunboats and patrol boats on inland rivers that were brown from soil runoff. Although small-boat operators were active in the Navy after this, it was not until 2006 that the Navy created the enlisted special boat operator position and career path. Today the main function of the SWCC continues to involve supporting and transporting SEALs and other special operations teams on oceans and rivers using surface boats. SWCC participate in the same missions these other teams undertake, such as counterterrorism, unconventional (guerrilla) warfare, foreign internal defense (training and helping the military forces of other countries fight against insurgents), direct action (striking at enemies), counterdrug operations, and special reconnaissance (covertly gathering information). Although SWCC are less well known than SEALs, one SEAL states on the Navy SEALs.com website that SWCC "are always the first to show up and the last to leave. Boat Guys are the unsung heroes of the Naval Special Warfare community."

SWCC drive 82-foot (25-m) MK-V special operations craft and 36-foot (11-m) rigid-hull inflatable boats on the ocean and 33-foot (10-m) special operations craft-riverine boats on rivers and in coastal ocean areas. These boats travel at high speeds, are designed to operate in extreme weather, and contain sophisticated communications gear, radar for detecting other vehicles, and weapons. Craft-riverine boats, for example, contain machine guns, miniguns, grenade launchers, GPS devices, and computerized detection gear that identifies boats or other vehicles. SWCC are tasked with protecting and defending themselves and others in or near their boats with these tools. For instance, in 1996 SWCC involved in counterdrug operations in Colombia were attacked in the Antioquia valley by about 150 Colombian guerrillas. The six SWCC fought valiantly for three days and nights, killing more than forty guerrillas and sustaining only one injury before other special forces teams arrived to assist them. The SWCC received medals for bravery and heroism.

Sometimes SWCC participate in nonmilitary missions. In July 2010, for example, SWCC who were in Philadelphia for Navy Appreciation Day celebrations heard a radio distress call from a tour boat that was struck by a barge. The boat sank, leaving thirty-seven people in the Delaware River. The SWCC mobilized their MK-V boat and arrived less than five minutes later to help police rescue the victims. Several SWCC pulled people onto their boat, and crewmen on a nearby pier pulled victims to safety using fire hoses.

How Do You Become a Navy Special Warfare Boat Operator?

Schooling, Group Activities, and Volunteer Work

Because SWCC often work in other countries, students interested in this career can benefit from foreign language, geography, political science, world or religious studies, and history classes that help them understand past and present wars and conflicts as well as other cultures. Physical fitness and teamwork are essential for SWCC, so participation in team sports is also beneficial. In fact, the military states that many special operations personnel participated in sports like lacrosse, water polo, swimming, track, football, and wrestling in high school. Participating in organizations such as Boy Scouts, which teach self-reliance, wilderness survival, first aid, and team-building skills, can also be helpful since SWCC often operate far away from civilization. Volunteer work in wilderness areas or in any capacity that develops organizational skills and requires interaction with people may also be beneficial.

Skills and Personality

SWCC must be dedicated to serving their country, physically fit, honorable, self-motivated, good team players, resilient, courageous, intelligent, and always striving to be better, in line with the section of the SWCC creed that states, "I challenge my brothers to perform, and I expect them to challenge me."

Qualifications

All SWCC are enlisted or warrant officer personnel. Candidates must initially join the Navy after taking the ASVAB, the pre-enlistment medical exam, and the Armed Forces Qualification Test. Applicants can also transfer into the Navy from another military branch.

Candidates need certain minimum scores on the verbal expression, arithmetic reasoning, and mechanical comprehension sections of the ASVAB to qualify for the SWCC. Next, they must pass the

PST, which tests swimming, running, and other physical fitness abilities. After the PST, candidates undergo the Computerized Special Operations Resilience Test (C-SORT), which evaluates mental resilience and emotional control. Candidates can only take the C-SORT once, but those who achieve a minimum PST score can begin training with an NSW mentor and later retake the PST. Applicants must achieve an optimum PST score to receive an SWCC contract. Examples of optimum scores are swimming 500 yards (457 m) using a sidestroke or breaststroke in 9.5 minutes, doing eighty push-ups in two minutes, and running 1.5 miles (2.4 km) in 10.5 minutes. Candidates must also pass a dive physical that shows they are able to dive.

Other SWCC qualifications include being male, a US citizen, between the ages of seventeen and thirty (although highly qualified candidates ages thirty to thirty-four may receive a waiver), eligible for a secret clearance, and having vision correctable to 20/25. Candidates also cannot be color blind, cannot have a felony conviction or substance abuse problems, and "must remain morally, mentally and physically qualified," according to the NSW Command.

Navy Training and Education

Those who qualify initially attend the eight-week NSW Preparation School, where candidates prepare for the rigorous physical training they will soon encounter. After passing a modified PST that includes swimming, running, and various other exercises, applicants proceed to a three-week NSW Orientation. During orientation they are further assessed for desirable characteristics and learn about the special operations lifestyle. Next is the seven-week Basic Crewman Training. About 240 active-duty sailors and 12 reservists start Basic Crewman Training each year, but fewer than half complete the course.

Candidates learn about and practice physical conditioning; water skills; small-boat navigation, maintenance, and repair; mental resilience; and teamwork during training. The major test of physical and mental strength occurs during a three-day exercise called "the Tour." During the Tour, candidates sleep very little and mostly stay outdoors swimming or on a boat. They also face navigation and combat challenges that require teamwork and tenacity to overcome. Those who pass go on to additional training in advanced navigation, marksmanship, and boat weapons and communications systems. During this phase, candidates also plan, prepare, and execute team missions and undergo training in survival-evasion-resistance-escape (SERE) techniques. SERE teaches personnel how to survive in any weather or environment if stranded, plus skills to avoid or deal with being captured by enemy forces.

Overall, each candidate travels about 3,200 nautical miles (5,926 km) in boats (with about 900 miles [1,667 km] occurring at night), swims 100 miles (161 km), runs 400 miles (644 km), performs 20,000 push-ups, and shoots 170,000 rounds of ammunition during SWCC training.

All SWCC candidates also attend a twelve-week language training course before they report for duty on a team, and all undergo combat medical training that includes emergency response, trauma medicine, water search and rescue, and medical evacuation. These skills are all important because SWCC often operate far away from medical facilities and must save the lives of teammates and other special forces operators. All SWCC have skills that are comparable to those of civilian EMTs. Some operators go on to attend advanced combat medical courses to achieve the designation of lead medic or independent duty corpsman. They are qualified to administer intravenous fluids and medicines, perform minor surgery, and intubate patients.

Many SWCC receive special training as parachutists as well. These men jump out of aircraft after inflatable boats attached to parachutes have been dropped. The SWCC land near the boats and, within about twenty minutes, can unpack and prepare them for a mission.

Once qualified as SWCC, operators are expected to constantly learn new skills and improve existing ones. They often take extra classes in communications, small-arms maintenance, military operations planning, and diesel engine maintenance.

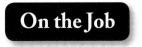

On the Job

Working Conditions

SWCC are stationed at navy bases in Coronado, California; Little Creek, Virginia; or Stennis, Mississippi. They can be deployed on missions to any of about thirty countries up to nine months per year. While deployed, SWCC might live in tents without electricity or running water in wilderness areas, deserts, or jungles, or they might live on allied military bases, among natives in a town, or on a ship.

SWCC often perform missions in hostile areas, infiltrating and exfiltrating other special forces teams to or from enemy beaches or transporting SEALs to intervene on boats involved in piracy, drug smuggling, or terrorism. For example, in April 2009 Somali pirates took over the civilian cargo ship *Maersk Alabama* in the Indian Ocean and held its captain, Richard Phillips, hostage on a lifeboat. SWCC and SEALs parachuted from an aircraft into the ocean near the USS *Bainbridge*, boarded the ship, and used it as a base of operations for their rescue mission. SEAL snipers on the *Bainbridge* killed the pirates, who held AK-47 weapons to Phillips's head, and SWCC whisked other SEALs to rescue Phillips in an inflatable boat.

On another mission, SWCC were tasked with the dangerous job of clearing the way for humanitarian aid supplies headed for the port city of Umm Qasr, Iraq, in 2003. The team achieved its mission by piloting MK-V boats down two nearby rivers. The crewmen navigated without charts in thick fog, rain, and sandstorms, all while dodging underwater mines and boat wreckages in which enemy soldiers hid.

Earnings

Monthly salary depends on pay grade and years of service. SWCC may also receive bonuses when they qualify as operators, as well as re-enlistment bonuses. They may be eligible for monthly hazardous duty pay of $150 to $340 for diving, $150 to $225 for parachuting, and up to $1,000 for speaking foreign languages, though there are limits on the number of special pays.

Opportunities for Advancement

SWCC regularly advance in rank on the basis of time served and can also be promoted for performance. Because all SWCC are enlisted men or petty officers, they have leadership opportunities not available to teams that are commanded by commissioned officers. For example, a first class petty officer (E-6) can be the officer in charge of his SWCC unit. This leadership experience often translates into advancement to positions of even greater responsibility and leadership in NSW or other departments.

What Is the Future Outlook for Navy Special Warfare Boat Operators?

The need for new SWCC should continue into the foreseeable future as special operations missions remain critical elements of military strategies around the world.

What Are Employment Prospects in the Civilian World?

With their training in boat operations and maintenance, parachuting, search and rescue, medical procedures, leadership, weapons, and mission planning, SWCC are well prepared for a variety of civilian careers. Many accept jobs in law enforcement, search and rescue, boat operations and repair, emergency medicine, and business. Many also go on to teach and train others in physical fitness, law enforcement, and other areas.

Marine Corps Force Recon

What Does the Marine Corps Force Recon Do?

At a Glance:
Marine Corps Force Recon

Minimum Educational Requirements
Enlisted: high school diploma; officers: bachelor's degree

Personal Qualities
Honorable, hardworking, self-motivated, committed to serving one's country, intelligent, adaptable, self-disciplined, physically fit

Certification and Licensing
Reconnaissance man qualified; reconnaissance man, parachutist qualified; reconnaissance man, combatant diver qualified

Working Conditions
Any environment: oceans, mountains, deserts, jungles, urban settings, airborne, battlefields

Salary Range
Monthly salary depends on pay grade and years of service

Number of Jobs
400 in 2015

Future Job Outlook
Continuing need for operators

The Marine Corps has long been considered to be the military's elite rapid response force, but special forces such as Force Reconnaissance (Force Recon) are handpicked ultra-elite teams. In fact, Marine Corps authorities report that commanders of other units are reluctant to allow soldiers selected for Force Recon to leave their units because they are the best of the best.

Reconnaissance involves observing and reporting on enemy actions and on geographic, cultural, social, and physical characteristics of areas in which military operations will take place. This includes reporting on roads, rivers, mountains, bridges, and towns. It may also involve assessing damage to troops and terrain after a battle. The Marine Corps Special Operations website calls Force Recon "the eyes and ears of the Marine Divisions."

Recon marines engage in water reconnaissance, which often includes scout swimming. Scout swimmers leave a boat before others on their raid team do and swim to shore to assess conditions on the beach. They may have to eliminate obstacles, including enemy forces, before it is safe for their team to land. Recon marines also perform land reconnaissance, which may involve secretly landing on a beach or parachuting deep into enemy territory before other troops arrive. Force Recon specializes in deep reconnaissance, in which operators go far behind enemy lines to gather information. For example, in 2001 and 2002 recon marines sneaked into Iraq and Afghanistan and used GPS devices and heat sensors to obtain information about the precise location of enemy troops and of target structures in mountain and desert areas and towns. They marked many targets with special laser markers that allow laser-guided missiles and bombs to find these targets. The marines transmitted this information to US commanders, who used it to plan their assault strategies.

Recon operators often deploy with Marine Expeditionary Units that travel on navy ships and engage in missions that involve small boats, close combat, demolitions (destroying dams or other enemy structures), maritime interdiction (intervening in events like piracy at sea), and boarding, searching, and seizing boats containing suspected terrorists or drug smugglers. They also perform other direct action missions, such as capturing terrorists, rescuing hostages, or raiding enemy countries' oil and gas platforms during conflicts. For example, in September 2010 recon operators stationed aboard the USS *Dubuque* in the pirate-infested Gulf of Aden received orders to free hostages taken by Somali pirates. The pirates had raided the German commercial ship *Magellan Star* and had announced they would not free the ship and its crew until they were paid a ransom. The marines quietly approached *Magellan Star* in small inflatable boats and boarded the ship. When the pirates found themselves suddenly faced with more than twenty weapons pointed at their faces, they surrendered immediately. The marines took the nine pirates as prisoners and freed the hostages with no shots fired, which is a primary recon goal. As Marine Corps officer Eric O'Neil writes in a *Forbes* magazine article, "Force Recon's mission is considered a success if absolutely no shots are fired."

Recon operators also protect high-ranking US military and civilian individuals when they visit hostile countries. For example, during recent wars in Iraq and Afghanistan, several operators provided protection for US military commanders and also trained foreign security experts in methods of protecting their own military leaders and politicians.

How Do You Become a Member of Force Recon?

Schooling, Group Activities, and Volunteer Work

Because recon operators often work in other countries, students interested in this type of career would benefit from foreign language, geography, political science, world or religious studies, and history classes that can help them understand past and present wars and conflicts and world cultures. Participation in ROTC to gain an understanding of how the military operates and trains its people can also be valuable. Because physical fitness and teamwork are essential to anyone who wishes to enter recon, students can also benefit from participation in team sports. In fact, the military states that many special forces members participated in sports like lacrosse, water polo, swimming, track, football, and wrestling in school. Participating in organizations such as Boy Scouts, which teach self-reliance, wilderness survival, and team-building skills, can also be helpful. Volunteer work in wilderness areas, with immigrant populations, or in any capacity that develops organizational skills and requires interaction with people may also be beneficial.

Skills and Personality

The book *Marine Force Recon*, by Fred J. Pushies, describes recon marines as "definitely Type-A personalities who believe if you're not living on the edge, you are taking up too much room!" Recon members often participate in triathlons and similar challenges just for fun and take pride in fulfilling the Force Recon creed, which states that recon marines "achieve what others can only imagine." Recon marines are intelligent, honorable, adaptable, hardworking, self-motivated, refuse to quit, and are committed to serving their country.

Qualifications

To be considered for Force Recon, candidates must join the Marine Corps as an officer or enlisted man, pass a physical exam, achieve a general technical score of 105 or higher on the ASVAB, pass a physical fitness test, possess a certification as a first-class swimmer, and have vision that can be corrected to 20/20. Applicants also cannot have any record of illegal drug use or mental health counseling. They must have at least eighteen months remaining on an enlistment contract after completing recon training, must be eligible for a secret clearance, must be a US citizen, and must have completed the marine infantry and rifleman courses.

After joining the Marine Corps and completing infantry training, the first step toward a recon career is undergoing a forty-eight-hour screening board. The assessment considers swimming ability, physical stamina, and psychological scores. Since the Marine Corps is an amphibious service, screeners view water skills as being especially important. Among other tests, candidates must perform an 82-foot (25-m) underwater swim, a deepwater rifle retrieval, and must tread water for thirty minutes. Fitness testing also involves an obstacle course as well as running 4 to 5 miles per hour (6- 8-kph) with a 50-pound (23-kg) rucksack. If a candidate fails or voluntarily drops out during the screening, he may reapply later on. The Marine Corps notes that many candidates fail several times before being accepted.

Marine Corps Training and Education

Enlisted candidates who are selected to continue are interviewed by a recon commander's company sergeant major or another noncommissioned officer. The recon commander himself interviews officers. Those who are selected after these interviews begin the indoctrination program, which includes physical fitness, team-building exercises, and learning about recon.

Next, candidates attend the Basic Reconnaissance Course, which takes place at a variety of military training schools, including the Army Airborne School and the Naval Diving Salvage and Training Center. It takes one and a half to two years to complete the schooling and training to become a qualified recon operator. The goal is to qualify in MOS 0321, which is the "reconnaissance man" qualification. When candidates also complete the Basic Airborne Course, this qualifies them as a reconnaissance man, parachutist qualified. Those who complete the Marine Corps Combatant Diver Course become a reconnaissance man, combatant diver qualified.

Recon training also includes advanced weapons, communications, engineering, and medical training and survival-evasion-resistance-escape (SERE) training. SERE teaches personnel how to survive in any weather or environment if stranded. It also teaches skills to avoid or deal with being captured by enemy forces since personnel who possess top-secret information are at high risk of being captured. Candidates must also complete the Mountain Leaders School and the Reconnaissance and Surveillance Leaders Course.

On the Job

Working Conditions

Force Recon missions may take place in any environment, including mountains, deserts, jungles, cities, battlefields, and at sea. While deployed, operators may live on bases, in homes among native populations, on navy ships, or in wilderness areas in tents without electricity or running water. Recon marines usually arrive at their missions via helicopter, small surface boat, navy ship, or submarine, and they may connect with these modes of transportation from a navy ship or from land.

Recon marines also do a great deal of swimming and diving to arrive at or conduct missions. When performing scout swimming, operators may jump from helicopters into ocean waters away from the shore, and must swim to shore without being spotted, or they may jump from small boats hundreds of yards offshore and swim the rest of the way. The job also involves sneaking ashore via piers or docks.

Although recon personnel strive to remain invisible while performing reconnaissance missions, they are still at high risk of being injured or captured by enemy forces because of the dangerous nature of operating behind enemy lines. For example, in 2004, recon teams infiltrated Fallujah, Iraq, before the historic battle in which US troops drove out guerrilla fighters. The marines hid in foxholes outside the city and in apartments and other hiding spots in town, including in garbage dumpsters, while obtaining information that allowed US forces to safely enter and take over two days later. Nonetheless, about half of these recon marines were wounded by Muslim guerrillas hiding in mosques and other buildings, and several were killed.

Despite these dangers, recon marines have a reputation for successfully obtaining needed information and remaining undetected because team members all look out for each other. As recon member Patrick Rogers explains in the publication the *Accurate Rifle*, "In Deep Reconnaissance, survival is based on stealth, and stealth is a by-product of [team] alertness."

Earnings

Monthly salary depends on pay grade and years of service. Recon marines may also receive monthly hazardous duty pay for diving (up to $340), parachuting ($150 to $225), and deployment ($50 to $300) and may also qualify for foreign language pay of up to $1,000 if they speak one or more foreign languages, though there are limits on the number of special pays.

Opportunities for Advancement

Recon operators advance in rank and pay rate regularly with time served and may also be promoted faster on the basis of performance. Many go on to screen and teach new operators or to lead departments in the Marine Corps or other branch of the military.

What Is the Future Outlook for Force Recon?

In 2015 the Marine Corps announced that it seeks to fill nearly eight hundred enlisted critical skills operator positions, which include Force Recon, over the next few years. But new recruits cannot join Force Recon until after they prove their expertise in weapons, combat, and other important skills. The officer in charge of screening and recruiting at Camp Lejeune, Captain William "Max" Wright, stated in a July 2015 *San Diego Union-Tribune* article that "it takes a long time to build to that number. . . . We are looking for experienced veterans. We don't take guys off the street."

What Are Employment Prospects in the Civilian World?

Many former recon operators work in law enforcement, including in organizations like the FBI and CIA. Many go on to accept jobs training and serving with civilian SWAT teams and federal marshals. Their skills also prepare them well for employment in search and rescue, boat operations, business, and as instructors in espionage and maritime operations. Many also work for firms that provide security and personal protection for dignitaries and executives.

Marine Corps Scout Snipers

What Does a Scout Sniper Do?

At a Glance:
Marine Corps Scout Snipers

Minimum Educational Requirements

High school diploma

Personal Qualities

Focused, intelligent, patient, able to work alone or with others, adaptable, able to make quick decisions, self-disciplined, able to function well under pressure, emotionally mature, physically fit

Certification and Licensing

Marine scout sniper specialist

Working Conditions

Any environment: oceans, deserts, forests, mountains, jungles, urban settings, aircraft, battlefields

Salary Range

Monthly salary depends on pay grade and years of service

Future Job Outlook

Continuing need for scout snipers

During conflicts it is often necessary to use snipers to disrupt the enemy's ability to fight. Snipers excel in targeting and shooting key enemy personnel and equipment from concealed locations. All soldiers are trained to shoot, but scout snipers undergo extra training in stalking and accurately targeting key military commanders, radio operators, and terrorists in the midst of crowded areas or over considerable distances. Snipers are also the best of the best at targeting enemy communications equipment, power generators, oil pipelines, and other assets. According to a Business Insider online article, scout snipers "can be more devastating on enemy forces than a plane full of bombs" because snipers carefully target their shots.

Snipers work in pairs to assist and protect each other. One sniper acts as the shooter and the other as the observer. The observer helps locate a target; calculates the effects of weather, wind, and moving targets; maintains both team members' equipment; and helps protect the shooter by staying alert for enemy soldiers, vehicles, and bombs as well as for natural threats such as dangerous animals.

Since the Marine Corps is an amphibious force, scout snipers often deploy with Marine Expeditionary Units on navy ships and conduct raids against ships, oil rigs, and shore targets. For example, on September 9, 2010, scout snipers on the USS *Dubuque* and on AH-1 helicopters overhead provided backup for a team of marine recon operators who boarded the German-owned commercial ship *Magellan Star* after Somali pirates took over and held the crew hostage in the Gulf of Aden. The recon marines were able to capture the pirates and free the *Magellan Star*'s crew with no shots fired, but the snipers were ready in case they were needed.

Snipers also use their skills on land-based battlefields. During the twenty-first century they have conducted missions in which they have stayed concealed for hours or days in rugged terrain or cities in Iraq and Afghanistan, tracking the movements of enemy fighters and taking action to stop their attacks on American forces. In one heroic shot in 2004 in Ramadi, Iraq, Scout Sniper Tim La Sage saved the lives of army personnel in a convoy by shooting the driver of an explosives-laden car when he observed the car heading right for the convoy. La Sage and his team were hidden on a balcony on the eighth floor of a building overlooking a crowded marketplace. They had been shooting enemy soldiers who were laying improvised explosive devices meant to kill American personnel when La Sage noticed the car and acted quickly.

Besides excelling in precision marksmanship, scout snipers also perform reconnaissance duties (observing and reporting on enemy actions and on geographic, social, and physical characteristics of areas in which military operations take place). Snipers excel in reconnaissance because they train with Force Recon teams and also because their training involves patiently observing targets for hours at a time while hidden. Snipers' high-tech spotting scopes allow them to see things many others would not notice, which enhances their reconnaissance abilities. For example, while observing a village marketplace, snipers would immediately notice an individual who looked nervous or out of place and would watch him or her as a potential terrorist.

How Do You Become a Scout Sniper?

Schooling, Group Activities, and Volunteer Work

Students considering a career as a scout sniper should strive for high academic and sports achievements and overall competitiveness in high school. Those who play team sports such as water polo, rugby, lacrosse, wrestling, or swimming in school have an especially good chance of being selected and succeeding in sniper jobs, where physical fitness and teamwork are critical. Taking classes in math, science, and English is important for helping students learn communications skills and the principles behind the science of shooting, which snipers must understand and use on the job. Since snipers work throughout the world, classes in foreign languages, geography, political science, history, and world cultures are also valuable. Participating in organizations such as Boy Scouts, which teach self-reliance, wilderness survival, and team-building skills, can also be helpful. Volunteer work in wilderness areas, with immigrant populations, or in any capacity that develops organizational skills and requires interaction with people may also be beneficial.

Skills and Personality

While excellent marksmanship is important for scout snipers, emotional and psychological stability, physical fitness and endurance, patience, and the ability to focus, make quick decisions, adapt to changing conditions, function well under pressure, and work well alone or with others are equally important. Another important quality is emotional maturity. The book *To Be a Military Sniper*, by Gregory Mast and Hans Halberstadt, explains that this quality is essential because it helps a sniper understand "the difference between when to shoot or not to shoot and the ability to live with the consequences of that decision."

Qualifications

After joining the Marine Corps and completing boot camp and infantry training, the next step toward a sniper career is to volunteer to undergo a forty-eight-hour scout sniper screening board. The assessment considers swimming ability, physical stamina, and psychological tests. Since the Marine Corps is an amphibious service, water skills are especially important. Among other skill tests, candidates must perform an 82-foot (25-m) underwater swim and deepwater rifle retrieval and must tread water for thirty minutes. Fitness testing also involves an obstacle course as well as running 4 to 5 miles per hour (6- to 8-kph) with a 50-pound (23-kg) rucksack. If a candidate fails or voluntarily drops out during the screening, he may reapply later on. The Marine Corps notes that many candidates fail several times before being accepted.

Candidates must also have the rank of E-3 through E-5 in the infantry, have vision that is correctable to 20/20, must score a minimum of 100 on the general technical category of the ASVAB, cannot have any history of mental illness, and may not have been court-martialed for at least six months. Other requirements include having at least twenty-four months remaining on one's Marine Corps contract after completing sniper training, and being certified as a rifle expert within one year of applying for the scout sniper position.

Marine Corps Training and Education

Qualified candidates must first become Force Recon specialists and serve in a recon battalion before they can apply for scout sniper school. After an interview with a recon commander's staff, those selected begin the recon indoctrination program. Those who pass the indoctrination must then complete the reconnaissance course before being assigned to a recon battalion. After serving on several recon deployments, a marine who wishes to become a scout sniper may volunteer and request enrollment in scout sniper school. Once enrolled, a sniper candidate's fellow marines label him a PIG (professionally instructed gunman). Those who go on to graduate are given the title of HOG (hunter of gunmen).

More than 60 percent of those who begin the eight-and-a-half-week-long sniper school drop out or are asked to leave because they cannot achieve the rigorous requirements. Those who finish become experts in stalking targets, concealment and camouflage, calculating wind and weather influences on shooting, estimating distances, using scopes and other tools, and firing sniper weapons. After training, snipers must be able to accurately hit a target up to 1,000 yards (914 m) away with an MK-11 sniper rifle and a target up to 1,800 yards (1,646 m) away—just over 1 mile (1.6 km)—with a .50-caliber rifle. In order to graduate, candidates must also demonstrate expertise in making themselves undetectable by others while stalking a target. Trainees therefore spend hours moving a few hundred yards without their instructors being able to detect them, either by seeing, hearing, or smelling them or by observing disturbances in the surrounding environment. Instructors stress that stalking skills and patience are as important as shooting skills. One instructor told *USA Today*, "Shooting is the easiest part of the job. It's more of a mental game than anything else."

Candidates also attend survival-evasion-resistance-escape (SERE) school to learn how to survive in any weather or environment if stranded. They are also taught skills to avoid or deal with being captured by enemy forces. Upon graduation from sniper school, personnel earn the

A US Marine Corps Scout Sniper, camouflaged for a winter training mission, prepares to fire his M40A3 bolt action sniper rifle as his spotter observes the target. Scout snipers target and shoot enemy personnel and equipment from concealed locations.

designation of scout sniper specialist. Each graduate receives a HOG tooth, which is a 7.62 millimeter bullet worn around the neck to go along with the HOG designation.

On the Job

Working Conditions

Sniper missions may occur anywhere in the world, from oceans and jungles to mountains, deserts, and even cities. Operators may live in military barracks, camp in tents without electricity or plumbing when out in wilderness areas, or live in houses or apartments in a town, depending on their mission. Snipers must often remain still and quiet in a concealed location—such as a hole in the ground, between boulders, in a tree, in an abandoned hut, or inside or atop an urban building— for hours or even days while observing the target. When snipers shoot, they may be sitting, standing, or lying down.

Shooter/observer teams must remain alert for changing conditions that might require them to change their position or attack plan. One way in which teams protect themselves is by wearing or hiding in different forms of camouflage and coloring their faces and hands to match their surroundings. The clothing they wear depends on their environment. In a forest, they wear clothing that blends in with trees and place clumps of grass or branches and leaves all over themselves. They do the same to hide their vehicles and tents. In a desert, their clothing blends in with sand. In snow conditions, snipers usually wear white camouflage suits and hoods with gray shading. In urban settings, snipers dress like the local inhabitants, including growing beards if this is prevalent in a particular location. It is critical for sniper teams to study their surroundings carefully before taking up a position, considering outsiders' views of their location from all angles, including front, back, and above; and to remain what the military calls *camouflage conscious* for the duration of the mission.

Earnings

Monthly salary depends on pay grade and years of service. Scout snipers may also be eligible for monthly special pay for hazardous duty

($50 to $300), parachuting ($150 to $225), diving ($150 to $340), and up to $1,000 for speaking one or more foreign languages, though there are limits on the number of special pays.

Opportunities for Advancement

Scout snipers regularly advance in rank and pay rate on the basis of time served. They can also advance because of performance to become team leaders, who are responsible for ensuring all their team members are trained and ready for missions. Since all scout snipers are enlisted, this gives them opportunities for leadership experience and positions that are reserved for officers in most units.

What Is the Future Outlook for a Scout Sniper?

In 2015 the Marine Corps announced that it was seeking to fill nearly eight hundred enlisted critical skills operator positions, which include scout snipers, over the next few years. Recruiting commanders emphasized that candidates must have extensive experience in the Marine Corps or other military branches before applying for these positions.

What Are Employment Prospects in the Civilian World?

With their training and skills, former scout snipers will find many civilian jobs open to them. Many former operators work for private security firms or law enforcement organizations, including in SWAT units or as intelligence specialists in private or public firms such as the FBI or CIA. Many teach and train law enforcement personnel or others who wish to learn to handle weapons.

Air Force Pararescue

At a Glance:
Air Force Pararescue

Minimum Educational Requirements
Enlisted: high school diploma or GED; officers: bachelor's degree

Personal Qualities
Intelligent, selfless, courageous, self-motivated, resilient, honorable, dedicated, adaptable, self-disciplined, able to function well under pressure, physically fit

Certification and Licensing
National Registry of Emergency Medical Technicians–Paramedic certification; certifications in high-altitude, low-opening parachuting and combat diving

Working Conditions
Any environment: mountains, deserts, jungles, oceans, battlefields, cities

Salary Range
Monthly salary depends on pay grade and years of service

Number of Jobs
About 500 in 2015

Future Job Outlook
Continuing need for pararescuemen

Air Force Pararescue originated in August 1943, when Lieutenant Colonel Donald Flickenger, Sergeant Harold Passey, and Corporal William McKenzie of the Army Air Force parachuted into a jungle in Burma to rescue a group of men who had bailed out of a disabled C-46 plane. After this, the military saw a need for specially trained pararescuemen, whose mission was to save lives. The program that trains medics known as parajumpers (PJs) to parachute into any environment to rescue injured or stranded soldiers officially launched in May 1946. Since then, PJs have saved lives in wartime and peacetime all over the world. Many PJs have received medals for heroic rescues in Korea, Vietnam, and subsequent wars, oftentimes ignoring their own wounds to help wounded soldiers. During the twenty-first century alone, PJs have performed more than twenty thousand combat and humanitarian rescues on land and sea.

There are currently about 500 PJs, whose teams include enlisted airmen and combat rescue officers (CROs). Their motto, So Others May Live, exemplifies their commitment to exposing themselves to danger and doing whatever else is needed to save lives. Pararescuemen often must kill or capture enemy soldiers to accomplish their mission, so they are well versed in combat skills as well as in saving lives.

A January 2012 incident highlights the dangers pararescuemen face. US special forces and Afghan commandos were fighting enemy forces in an Afghan village, and an Afghan soldier was severely wounded. Air force pilots immediately flew to the scene with a team of PJs in two Pave Hawk helicopters. One copter had to land in an exposed riverbed where it was vulnerable to attack, so the other aircraft hovered to protect it. As copilot Brian Stroud revealed in an *Air Force News* article, "One thing different about this mission was that since we were at the bottom of a river valley . . . if we were engaged [by gunfire] we were completely helpless." The PJs sped to rescue the wounded man; once they had stabilized his condition, they sped back to the aircraft, carrying him on a stretcher. The team later received the Mackay Trophy, which honors air force personnel who exhibit bravery in extremely dangerous situations.

PJs also go to great lengths to save civilians. In 2014, for example, four PJs from the 129th Rescue Wing (an air force reserve unit) parachuted from a helicopter carrying a raft to save a sick toddler who was aboard a sailboat in the Pacific Ocean 900 miles (1,448 km) east of Mexico.

Unlike the publicity that surrounds other special operations teams like the Green Berets and the SEALs, PJs are not well known and prefer to keep it that way. Over half of all Air Force Cross recipients are in Pararescue, but the public is largely unaware that these teams even exist.

How Do You Become a Pararescueman?

Schooling, Group Activities, and Volunteer Work

Students interested in becoming a pararescueman should strive for high academic and sports achievements and overall competitiveness in high school. Those who play team sports such as water polo, rugby, lacrosse, wrestling, swimming, or boxing in school have an especially good chance of being selected and succeeding in pararescue jobs, where physical fitness and teamwork are critical. Taking classes in math, science, and English is important for helping students learn communications skills and principles behind emergency medicine and aviation. Since pararescuemen are sent throughout the world, classes in foreign languages, geography, political science, history, and world cultures are also valuable.

Participation in ROTC to gain an understanding of how the military operates and trains its people can also be valuable. Organizations such as Boy Scouts, which teach self-reliance, wilderness survival, and team-building skills, can also be helpful. Volunteer work in wilderness areas, with organizations that practice emergency medicine, or in any capacity that develops organizational skills and requires interaction with people may also be beneficial.

Skills and Personality

The Air Force seeks airmen who are intelligent, selfless, courageous, self-motivated, resilient, honorable, dedicated, adaptable, self-disciplined, able to function well under pressure, and physically fit to become PJs. Skills in skiing, rock climbing, swimming, and scuba diving—which all pararescuemen must learn—may be advantageous in qualifying for this career.

Qualifications

Prospective pararescuemen must be male, US citizens, and able to obtain a secret security clearance, and must have vision correctable to 20/20. They must join the Air Force before their twenty-eighth birthday and must be between 5 feet and 6 feet 8 inches (152.5 to 203.2 cm) tall. Candidates must not weigh more than 250 pounds (113 kg), cannot be color blind, and must not have a record of felony convictions or substance abuse. Candidates must also pass the Physical Ability and Stamina Test, achieving a minimum of being able to swim 82 feet (25 m) underwater two times; swimming 1,640 feet (500 m) in 10 minutes, 7 seconds or less; running 1.5 miles (2 km) in 9 minutes, 47 seconds or less; and performing other tests of strength and endurance. They must also pass a flight physical exam and numerous psychological tests. Prospective CROs must also pass the one-week-long Officer Selection Course before beginning CRO training.

Air Force Training and Education

The two-year-long PJ training program, known as the Pipeline or Superman School, is among the toughest in the special forces. Indeed, only 10 to 20 percent of those who begin training finish.

The first step in pararescue training is to pass the Pararescue/Combat Rescue Officer Indoctrination Course. This involves physical fitness tests in running, swimming, weight training, and calisthenics, along with training in medical procedures, weapons, and leadership. Candidates then take hands-on courses at combat dive school to learn scuba diving, other methods of water infiltration, and methods of rescuing people in water. Next comes Army Airborne School to learn several types of parachuting and survival-evasion-resistance-escape (SERE) training to teach airmen how to survive in any weather or environment if stranded. SERE also teaches skills to avoid or deal with being captured by enemy forces. Paramedic school, which teaches medical emergency treatments, drug administration, and basic surgeries, is next. Candidates then learn advanced parachuting techniques and methods for escaping from an aircraft that crash lands in water. After completing these courses, enlisted PJs are assigned to a pararescue team for on-the-job training. CROs proceed to the seventeen-week-long CRO Apprentice Course.

Some of the more challenging aspects of the Pipeline include parachuting into the ocean at night from an elevation of 26,000 feet (7,925 m) while in full combat gear and carrying scuba tanks that can weigh up to 170 pounds (77 kg). Candidates are also left alone in many environments for days, tasked with avoiding instructors who pretend to be enemy forces. They also practice rescuing injured people by climbing steep cliffs, venturing inside collapsed and smoldering buildings, and while dangling from a wire attached to a hovering helicopter. The Air Force says this grueling training is necessary because lives are at stake, and pararescuemen must learn to quickly adapt to any conditions.

Those who complete the Pipeline and graduate are awarded the prestigious maroon beret with the Air Force Pararescue flash insignia.

During a 2015 exercise, US Air Force Pararescue jumpers from the 920th Rescue Wing practice search-and-rescue techniques that would be used in large-scale flooding. Pararescue parajumpers perform combat and humanitarian rescues on land and sea.

The color represents the blood PJs have shed during their missions. Graduates also receive the National Registry of Emergency Medical Technicians–Paramedic certification and certifications in high-altitude, low-opening parachuting and combat diving.

On the Job

Working Conditions

The military formally designates pararescuemen as *personnel recovery specialists*. In line with this job title, they are called upon to rescue and administer emergency medical aid or to recover deceased soldiers' bodies at any hour of the day or night, in every conceivable type of environment. Although pararescuemen usually live on military bases while deployed, they are ready to launch at a moment's notice.

Pararescuemen can reach their destinations by jumping or fast-roping from a helicopter over land or sea, parachuting from a fixed-wing plane, swimming or scuba diving, or rock climbing. They also may use skis, snowmobiles, ATVs, motorcycles, military vehicles, jet skis, or boats. Since they never know which equipment they will need on a mission, they carry all of these modes of transportation, along with many medical supplies and weapons, in the aircraft or boats in which they deploy. Once they arrive on a mission, they are wilderness and battlefield survival experts who help others, as well as themselves, survive until an evacuation can take place. While on a mission, para-rescuemen may live in a tent without electricity or running water, in a building if one is available, in a boat, or anywhere else until they and their patients make it to a military base or hospital.

In recent years PJs have entered a variety of hazardous situations to perform their job. They have rescued many people off the coast of Africa while challenged with avoiding pirates, sharks, and heavy ocean currents. In other dangerous conditions, PJs have braved temperatures of -40°F (-40°C), heavy winds, and possible gunfire from enemy soldiers to rescue more than three hundred Afghan civilians who were stranded in a mountain pass after thirty-six avalanches struck the area in February 2010. Pararescuemen have also parachuted onto battle-fields during recent wars in Iraq and Afghanistan to treat wounded soldiers while bullets and bombs exploded around them. Many PJs have been injured or killed this way. Their job of rescuing soldiers be-came even more dangerous after enemy forces began setting search-and-rescue traps—bombs placed to specifically target medics and search-and-rescue teams.

Some missions are achieved quickly, in under an hour, but others may take days or weeks. For example, after Hurricane Katrina devastated areas in the southern United States in 2005, PJs fast-roped from hovering helicopters and swam through polluted water while rescuing more than one thousand people over several weeks' time.

Earnings

Monthly salary depends on pay grade and years of service. Pararescue-men may also be eligible for special monthly hazardous duty pay, which may include flight pay ($110 to $200), dive pay ($150), parachute pay ($110 to $225), foreign language pay up to $1,000, and other special duty pay ($55 to $165), though there are limits on the number of special pays. Personnel may also receive reenlistment bonuses.

Opportunities for Advancement

Personnel advance in rank and pay grade on the basis of time served, and some are promoted early for excellent performance or for receiving a medal. The Air Force also offers accelerated promotions for those who initially enlist for six years. Many pararescuemen go on to teach and train new pararescuemen as well as to serve in administrative or military command positions.

What Is the Future Outlook for Pararescuemen?

The need for new pararescuemen should continue into the foreseeable future as special operations missions remain critical elements of military strategies around the world.

What Are Employment Prospects in the Civilian World?

Many former pararescuemen become civilian paramedics or work in law enforcement and/or search and rescue after leaving the military. Many go on to teach and train others who are entering these fields as well. Some become personal trainers or work in other aspects of physical fitness.

Air Force Combat Control

At a Glance:
Air Force Combat Control

Minimum Educational Requirements
Enlisted: high school diploma or GED; officers: bachelor's degree

Personal Qualities
Intelligent, courageous, honorable, self-confident yet humble, disciplined, self-motivated, dedicated, resilient, adaptable, physically fit

Certification and Licensing
FAA-certified air traffic controller; certified joint terminal attack controller; certifications in high-altitude, low-opening parachuting and combat diving

Working Conditions
Any environment: battlefields, mountains, jungles, deserts, towns, cities, ocean

Salary Range
Monthly salary depends on pay grade and years of service

Number of Jobs
About 1,500 in 2015

Future Job Outlook
Continuing need for combat controllers

Civilian air traffic controllers direct aircraft in, around, and between airports. The Air Force's fifteen hundred special operations combat controllers also direct air traffic, but their jobs do not end there. Combat controllers, who can be enlisted airmen or special tactics officers, are certified through the Federal Aviation Association (FAA) as air traffic controllers and are also experts in planning and executing special reconnaissance and combat missions. One of their biggest roles is scouting air targets and gathering intelligence on many factors before other military teams arrive for a war or battle. The combat controller motto, First There, refers to the role controllers play in paving the way for other units in war zones.

To do their jobs, combat controllers rely on sophisticated tools. For example, in the wars in Iraq and Afghanistan during the 1990s through early twenty-first century, combat controllers infiltrated these areas and marked air targets with laser finders, reflectors, and radar beacons to guide laser-guided missiles and other types of weapons to these targets. Combat controllers also marked airstrips and runways in the Iraqi desert with portable infrared lights and took soil samples to determine which types of aircraft could safely land.

Other jobs combat controllers perform before other troops arrive include surveying and assessing the best places for triage and medical evacuations. They also locate refueling areas for aircraft and other vehicles. These jobs require them to take photographs and draw sketches of bridges, roads, and other assets to send to military commanders. Combat controllers also demolish any structures that might interfere with US missions, and they set up semipermanent radio and other communications links, and place sensors in various places to detect and remotely report on enemy personnel, aircraft, ground vehicles, missile launchers, and bomb storage sites.

Once a war commences, combat controllers fight alongside and support other special operations teams, such as Air Force Pararescuemen, Army Green Berets, and Navy SEALs, by calling in air support to protect these teams. Most combat controllers are certified as joint terminal attack controllers as well as air traffic controllers, which allows them to call in and direct bombing raids and other air attacks while directing air traffic. During the war in Afghanistan from 2001 to 2015, for example, combat controllers called in about 85 percent of the air strikes. In 2003, in one battle in which enemy fighters ambushed a special operations group, Combat Control technical sergeant Kevin Whalen was hit by enemy gunfire. Whalen kept shooting and killed numerous assailants until enemy fire destroyed his weapon. He then retreated into his vehicle to bandage his wound while calling in air support and medical aid. When medical teams arrived, he continued to direct air traffic and refused to be evacuated until all of his team members were safe. Whalen was awarded the Silver Star for his actions.

Like the special forces teams to which they are attached, combat controllers are involved in counterterrorism, foreign internal defense (helping and training other countries' military forces to fight against insurgents), and search-and-rescue missions. Combat controllers also participate in humanitarian relief operations. For instance, after a devastating earthquake struck Haiti on January 12, 2010, a Combat

Control team stationed at Hurlburt Field, Florida, received word that hundreds of aircraft headed for Toussaint Louverture International Airport in Port-au-Prince to deliver humanitarian aid could not land because the earthquake had disabled the control tower and radio communications. The team, led by Chief Master Sergeant Tony Travis, immediately flew to Haiti and set up a folding card table near the airport runway. For two weeks, they used handheld radios to direct the take-offs and landings of more than four thousand aircraft from all over the world. They also rode motorcycles to lead the planes to parking places. *Time* magazine recognized Travis as one of the one hundred most influential people of 2010, despite Travis's statement to the *Air Force Times* that "they gave me credit for the men and women who worked for me."

How Do You Become a Member of Combat Control?

Schooling, Group Activities, and Volunteer Work

Students interested in Combat Control should strive for high academic and sports achievements and overall competitiveness in high school. Those who play team sports such as water polo, rugby, lacrosse, wrestling, or swimming have an especially good chance of being selected for Combat Control, where physical fitness and teamwork are critical. Taking classes in math, science, and English is important for helping students learn communication skills and the principles behind aviation. Since combat controllers are sent throughout the world, classes in foreign languages, geography, political science, history, and world cultures are also valuable. Participation in ROTC to gain an understanding of how the military operates and trains its people can also be valuable. Organizations such as Boy Scouts, which teach self-reliance, wilderness survival, and team-building skills, can also be helpful. Volunteer work in wilderness areas, with immigrant populations, or in any capacity that develops organizational skills and requires interaction with people may also be beneficial.

Skills and Personality

Combat Control teams need personnel who are intelligent, courageous, self-confident yet humble, disciplined, resilient, self-motivated, and physically fit. In addition, "To do what they do takes not only advanced training and intelligence but also a daring sense of adventure," explains technical sergeant Chris Rabenold in an Air Force Technical Degree Sponsorship Program video. Skills in skiing, rock climbing, swimming, and scuba diving, which all combat controllers must learn, can also be advantageous for candidates.

Qualifications

Combat Control candidates must be male, US citizens, FAA-certified air traffic controllers, have normal color vision and vision that is correctable to 20/20, must pass a medical exam and a flight physical, and must join the Air Force before age twenty-eight. Candidates must also be between 4 feet 10 inches (147 cm) and 6 feet 8 inches (203.2 cm) tall and weigh a maximum of 250 pounds (113 kg). They must meet minimum standards on the Physical Ability and Stamina Test, such as swimming 1,640 feet (500 m) in 11 minutes, 42 seconds or less and running 1.5 miles (2 km) in 10 minutes, 10 seconds or less. Enlisted candidates must achieve certain minimum ASVAB scores in the general, mechanical, administrative, and electrical sections.

Air Force Training and Education

Combat controller training is among the toughest special forces training programs. Only 10 to 20 percent of those who begin training finish the two-year program. Candidates must maintain their air traffic control certification while training and becoming proficient in combat, infiltration, and other necessary skills.

Combat controller selection and training begin with a two-week course that introduces Combat Control history and focuses on exercise and sports physiology, nutrition, and physical fitness. Then comes the Combat Control Operator Course, which focuses on aircraft recognition and performance, air navigation, weather, traffic control, and communications. At the Army Airborne School, candidates learn basic parachuting skills before proceeding to the Air Force Basic Survival School, which teaches candidates how to survive in any climate and geographic area. Next, Combat Control School focuses on small-unit tactics, land navigation, demolitions, fire support, advanced parachuting, and more physical fitness training. Those who graduate receive the prestigious scarlet beret with the Combat Control insignia. The color represents the blood combat controllers have shed to accomplish their missions.

After graduating, combat controllers enroll in Special Tactics Advanced Skills Training. Here, they learn about and practice operational readiness and mission planning and are again pushed to their mental and physical limits with constant physical challenges. These include marches carrying heavy rucksacks, running seven-minute miles, and endless calisthenics. Combat controllers also attend the Army's military freefall parachuting school and the Air Force's combat dive school to earn certifications in high-altitude, low-opening parachuting and combat diving. Most also undergo special training to become certified as joint terminal attack controllers.

On the Job

Working Conditions

Combat controllers can work in any environment—mountains, battlefields, jungles, deserts, and cities—and in any type of weather—snow, rain, scorching heat, and sandstorms. While deployed, they often live on a military base in barracks or in semipermanent tents, but they also may be stuck atop a mountain outside an enemy city for days, either alone or with a team, controlling air traffic and sleeping in a tent or other primitive structure without electricity or running water. Sometimes combat controllers hide in dugouts or among trees for weeks at a time while performing special reconnaissance in hostile areas. Oftentimes, some team members stand guard while others sleep.

Combat controllers may arrive at their mission sites by air, land, or sea, so they are well versed in operating all types of aircraft, boats, jet skis, submarines, motorcycles, ATVs, snowmobiles, and trucks. They are also experts in parachuting, fast-roping, rapelling, rock climbing, skiing, scuba diving and other amphibious infiltration techniques, and navigating anywhere using only a map and compass if necessary. When marking airfields and scouting targets, combat controllers often parachute into an area along with dirt bikes, which are also attached to parachutes. They then ride the dirt bikes while scouting and clearing away obstacles to prepare the airfields for US aircraft landings.

Despite all of the hardships and dangers, combat controllers, like other special operations personnel, are trained to selflessly do their jobs without quitting or abandoning their teammates. In one dramatic case in Afghanistan in 2009, Combat Controller Robert Gutierrez's team came under heavy fire while pursuing a terrorist. When Gutierrez was shot through the chest, his lung collapsed and he started coughing up blood. He thought he had three minutes to live before bleeding out, and he vowed to save his teammates in the meantime. He continued to direct air traffic, called in fighter planes, and kept firing at enemy forces while a medic repeatedly reinflated his lung with a 7-inch (18 cm) needle. His actions saved the lives of nearly thirty teammates before he became unconscious. Gutierrez spent nearly two years recovering in a hospital, and in 2011 he received the Air Force Cross for his heroism. He later told the *San Diego Union-Tribune* that his teammates "would have all done the same thing. . . . They would just would never quit."

Earnings

Monthly salary depends on pay grade and years of service. Combat controllers also may be eligible for monthly hazardous duty pay of $110 to $225 for parachuting, $110 to $200 for flight pay, $150 for dive pay, $150 for demolitions, $55 to $165 for special duty pay, and up to $1,000 for speaking foreign languages, though there are limits on the number of special pays. Personnel may also be eligible for reenlistment bonuses. In fact, Combat Control reenlistment bonuses are the highest in the military because not many airmen wish to train for or stay in this dangerous specialty, making it an undermanned position according to the military.

Opportunities for Advancement

Combat controllers receive regular promotions in rank and pay grade according to time served, though controllers often have faster promotion rates than normal due to performance. Many combat controllers, such as Gutierrez, go on to teach and train Combat Control candidates, and some advance to high-ranking positions in the Air Force or the rest of the military.

What Is the Future Outlook for Combat Controllers?

The need for new combat controllers should continue into the foreseeable future as special operations missions remain critical elements of military strategies around the world. The military offers incentive and reenlistment bonuses to help entice qualified personnel to apply for Combat Control.

What Are Employment Prospects in the Civilian World?

With their combat, reconnaissance, survival, fitness, and organizational skills, a wide range of civilian jobs are open to combat controllers. Many go on to work as civilian air traffic controllers. Some pursue jobs in law enforcement, including careers with the FBI and CIA. Still others find employment with private security firms, in search and rescue, as fitness trainers, as law enforcement or aviation instructors, and in business careers.

Coast Guard Maritime Safety and Security Team

At a Glance:
Coast Guard Maritime Safety and Security Team

Minimum Educational Requirements
Enlisted: high school diploma or GED; officers: bachelor's degree

Personal Qualities
Intelligent, courageous, honorable, self-confident yet humble, disciplined, self-motivated, dedicated, resilient, adaptable, physically fit

Certification and Licensing
Enlisted: maritime enforcement specialist A; officers: MSST deployable team leader, MSST boarding officer

Working Conditions
Ports, oceans, rivers, coastal areas on boats or aircraft

Salary Range
Monthly salary depends on pay grade and years of service

Number of Jobs
About 900 in 2015

Future Job Outlook
Ongoing need for operators

What Does the Coast Guard Maritime Safety and Security Team Do?

On September 11, 2001, Coast Guard personnel were among the first responders after terrorists flew planes into the World Trade Center in New York City. They helped evacuate more than five hundred thousand people in boats. Because of its importance in national security, in 2002 the Coast Guard became part of the Department of Homeland Security as well as a branch of the Department of Defense. The Coast Guard then created the special operations Maritime Safety and Security Team (MSST) and several other units to expand its role in national security.

The MSST patrols and enforces security measures in US

ports and waterways and along coastlines to achieve its primary mission of stopping terrorists, drug smugglers, and illegal immigrants before they reach the United States. The MSST also protects American interests in water areas elsewhere in the world. Other military branches like the Navy, with whom the MSST often works, cannot act against or arrest people for violating US laws. But the Coast Guard's unique authority as both a military and a civil law enforcement service allows the MSST to perform atypical operations. For instance, in 2012, a navy helicopter squadron based at Mayport, Florida, was tasked with finding and stopping drug runners in US waters in the Gulf of Mexico. Since navy personnel cannot board and search boats in US waters, their helicopter teams included Coast Guard marksmen, who fired warning shots or disabled the drug runners' boat engines with bullets, boarded the boats, and arrested the drug runners.

The MSST usually patrols and conducts missions using Coast Guard boats, aircraft, or land vehicles. Besides boarding and searching boats or shoreline facilities suspected of involvement with illegal or terrorist activities, the MSST is also responsible for inspecting commercial ships that enter US ports and for stopping divers and swimmers who intend to do harm. The MSST uses detection equipment such as the Underwater Port Security System, which can be mounted on small boats or piers, to scan underwater areas with poor visibility. The system employs sonar and can distinguish divers from sea life and structures. When necessary, the MSST uses an underwater weapons system called the Integrated Anti-Swimmer System, which emits shockwaves to stun or force malicious divers or swimmers to surface.

Other MSST jobs include protecting US military personnel on ships leaving or entering the United States, enforcing security at maritime events like boat races, and performing search-and-rescue missions for stranded or injured boaters or swimmers. In addition, MSST personnel are involved in what the Coast Guard publication titled *Doctrine for the US Coast Guard* calls "protecting the sea itself" from environmental and human-made threats such as oil spills and illegal overfishing. The MSST achieves this job through law enforcement and education campaigns.

How Do You Become a Member of the Maritime Safety and Security Team?

Schooling, Group Activities, and Volunteer Work

Students interested in the MSST should strive for high academic and sports achievements in high school. Those who play team sports such as water polo, rugby, lacrosse, wrestling, or swimming have an especially good chance of being selected for MSST jobs, where physical fitness and teamwork are critical. Taking classes in math, science, English, and pre-law can help students learn communication skills and the scientific and legal principles behind MSST careers. Since MSST personnel are sent throughout the world, classes in foreign languages, geography, political science, history, and world cultures are also valuable.

Participation in ROTC to gain an understanding of how the military operates and trains its people can also be valuable. Organizations such as Boy Scouts, which teach self-reliance, wilderness survival, and team-building skills, can also be helpful. Volunteer work in any capacity that develops organizational skills and requires interaction with people may also be beneficial.

Skills and Personality

MSST candidates must be intelligent, courageous, honorable, self-confident yet humble, disciplined, self-motivated, dedicated, resilient, adaptable, and physically fit. They need strong leadership and teaching skills and must have a strong interest in law enforcement and security.

Qualifications

The MSST accepts females as well as males. Coast Guard officers who wish to be considered for the MSST must inform their command of this goal, must demonstrate successful leadership in their jobs after being commissioned, and must be certified as Coast Guard boarding team members. Enlisted candidates should request a maritime enforcement (ME) specialty during basic training and must have a minimum ASVAB score of 100 on the verbal expression and arithmetic reasoning sections. They also must have at least two years of service remaining on their original service contract after completing MSST training.

All candidates must be US citizens, eligible for a secret clearance, must possess a valid driver's license, may not be color blind, must have vision correctable to 20/20, and must not be taking any medications that could impair judgement or reflexes. Applicants must also not have any history of drug or alcohol abuse, may not have domestic violence convictions or restraining orders that prevent them from legally carrying a firearm, and must not have been court-martialed. In addition, candidates must comply with Coast Guard weight and body fat standards and must pass either the Boarding Officer and Boat Crew Physical Fitness Test or the Deployable Specialized Forces Tier II Physical Fitness Test. Both of these tests assess a candidate's ability to achieve certain requirements for sit-ups, push-ups, sit-and-reach exercises, swimming, and running. These fitness requirements depend on age and gender. For example, men under age thirty must run 1.5 miles (2 km) in 12 minutes, 51 seconds or less. Women under age thirty must run 1.5 miles (2 km) in 15 minutes, 26 seconds or less.

Coast Guard Training and Education

MSST candidates begin training at the ten-week Maritime Enforcement Specialist "A" School, where they learn how to provide security and law enforcement support for Coast Guard missions. Schooling also emphasizes leadership, physical fitness, weapons, antiterrorism, port readiness, tactical operations, and communications training. Candidates also undergo extensive weapons training and additional physical fitness training at the Federal Law Enforcement Training Centers (FLETC). FLETC training also includes an antiterrorism program that trains candidates to board and search commercial sea vessels and teaches advanced skills for operating boats at high speeds while enforcing maritime security.

The eight-week Basic Tactical Operations Course is next. This course prepares candidates for the high-risk missions in which they will participate. It includes classroom instruction and real-world drills in advanced interdiction (disrupting or preventing certain illegal acts) and counterterrorism skills, including marksmanship, close-quarters combat, and breaching (forcibly opening doors or otherwise gaining access when necessary). Students must pass this course with a GO (criteria are GO or NO GO) to qualify for the MSST.

Officer candidates are also required to pass the Maritime Law Enforcement Course and the Boarding Officer Practical Course, both of which emphasize the legal aspects of maritime law enforcement. The officer training program is evolving, and it is unknown how it will change in the future.

After passing all of these courses, MSST trainees engage in on-the-job training that involves simulated scenarios they are likely to encounter. For example, in 2014 a reporter with the Northwest Military.com news service rode along in a small boat with MSST trainer James Moerls on a training exercise in the Seattle Harbor. Moerls suddenly aimed his boat at a pier. The reporter wrote, "In this scenario, our boat was a waterborne improvised explosive device racing over the dark water toward a restaurant on the end of the pier." The MSST trainees in four Coast Guard response boats calmly closed in on Moerls's boat to make it stop. Another trainer commented that the trainees are "capable of any mission the Coast Guard throws at them."

On the Job

Working Conditions

MSST personnel can be stationed in the United States or around the world to patrol and protect maritime areas in which there are known or suspected threats to the United States. Many are stationed on military bases in the United States. Some live in base housing, but most live in private homes. While working in their home ports, MSST personnel patrol and conduct missions using Coast Guard cutters or patrol boats, small speedboats, motorized lifeboats, maritime patrol aircraft, and shore patrol vehicles. These boats are all designed to operate in heavy surf or adverse weather conditions, but operators still risk their lives when they venture out to sea in storms that other boats and ships try to avoid by sheltering in port.

Many times, MSST personnel deploy aboard navy ships for six months or more and use cutters or helicopters based on these ships to patrol or conduct enforcement or rescue missions out on the ocean. They often pilot a Coast Guard cutter stored on a navy ship to intercept or rescue people on another boat. Other times, MSST members may fast-rope from helicopters onto ships or boats that they must board to stop illegal activities.

Other deployments may occur closer to home and may involve going from the team's home port to another port on cutters or patrol boats. For example, in 2012 an MSST stationed at Kings Bay, Georgia, deployed to New Jersey to support security and safety efforts after Hurricane Sandy devastated the shore area. The team set up a base on the shore and used their cutters and patrol boats to help local authorities patrol and evacuate people for several weeks.

MSST personnel also frequently travel from their home ports to engage in antiterrorism, anti–drug smuggling, and other types of law enforcement and water safety training exercises with US or foreign navies and port security teams. In one exercise in June 2015 in Port Angeles, Washington, MSST crews from Port Angeles, Seattle, and San Diego worked alongside teams from the US Navy and the Royal Canadian Navy. The teams deployed on helicopters and small boats to conduct a variety of simulated boarding exercises. In one drill, they boarded a ship that had supposedly experienced a crew mutiny. In another scenario, they took over a boat containing illegal immigrants, and still another exercise involved coordinating a rescue mission after reaching a boat whose crew had reported that a man had fallen overboard. These exercises help MSST personnel stay ready for anything that may occur.

Earnings

Monthly salary depends on pay grade and years of service. MSST personnel can also receive special sea pay of $100 per month, overseas housing allowances based on location, dive pay of $150 to $340 per month, foreign language proficiency pay of $100 to $300 per month, hardship duty pay of $50 to $150 per month, special pay for duty subject to hostile force or imminent danger of $225 per month, hazardous duty incentive pay of $150 per month, and aviation pay of $125 to $585 per month, depending on years of service, for flying or being a crew member on an aircraft. There are limits on how many special pays each MSST member can receive.

Opportunities for Advancement

Officer and enlisted MSST personnel regularly advance in rank on the basis of time served. They can also be promoted early on the basis of exceptional leadership, expertise, and job performance.

What Is the Future Outlook for the Coast Guard Maritime Safety and Security Team?

About twenty-five officers are accepted into the MSST training program each year, and it is unknown how this may change in the future. However, with the ongoing need for antiterrorism and law enforcement teams in the United States and abroad, the need for new enlisted personnel and officers should continue in the foreseeable future.

What Are Employment Prospects in the Civilian World?

With extensive skills and knowledge in law enforcement, maritime law, maritime combat, boat and aircraft operations, and leadership, there are a variety of civilian job areas in which former MSST personnel can find work and excel. Civilian law enforcement departments, private port security firms, boat operations and maintenance businesses, and teaching positions in law enforcement are just a few of the many jobs that welcome former members of the MSST.

Interview with a Green Beret

Major Anthony Aguilar is an Army Green Beret who is currently deployed to Dushanbe, Tajikistan, where he is in charge of coordinating Army Special Forces missions and serving as a liaison to the US embassy. After graduating from the US Military Academy at West Point, New York, he served as an infantry officer for three years before qualifying as a Green Beret in 2008. Aguilar spoke with the author about his military career.

Q: Why did you join the Army?

A: My desire was to attend West Point so I could serve my country and also have the military pay for my college education. I didn't plan to make it a long-term career, but after I received my commission and realized I gained satisfaction from contributing to making the world a better place, I decided to stay. Now I'm in it for the long haul.

Q: Why did you become a Green Beret?

A: Mainly for the challenge and excitement of being part of an elite force and for the opportunity to do things most people don't get to do. As a Green Beret you are deployed to parts of the world no one else in the military gets to go to, and you have the opportunity to do a range of challenging missions. Another big plus is the camaraderie. I get to work with great people I can trust and depend on.

Q: How did you train to become a Green Beret?

A: The training program is long and challenging. We were trained in combat, leadership, physical fitness, weapons, technical issues, how to negotiate, how to plan and execute operations. There was foreign language training, intelligence training, training in managing mission finances, and survival training so you can survive on your own or with a team wherever you may be. The training is tough because you are being trained to be a flexible, adaptive individual who can go into and succeed in any situation anywhere in the world, whether in a hut in the jungle or in an office at headquarters. When you finish your training you are ready for anything, no matter how challenging. You have learned that you are responsible for yourself and your team and that if you don't do something, it won't get done, because in the Green Berets there is no one standing over you, making sure you do things right.

Q: Please describe a typical Green Beret workday.

A: There are no typical workdays. Every day is different. One day I might be planning details of a mission or arranging for supplies for my unit, and the next day I might be meeting with the leader of Tajikistan to coordinate our joint missions. Then I might travel to begin a mission or travel to brief the secretary of defense on one of our missions, or I might be doing the training in artillery or parachuting or other skills we constantly train in to keep ourselves ready. Each mission is different too. I have been on many different types of missions—drug-related, law enforcement, combat, sensitive operations, or diplomacy. I've worked with commandos in Afghanistan and headquarters officers in the Philippines, and no two days are alike.

Q: What do you like most and least about being a Green Beret?

A: What I like most is the personal satisfaction I get from my job. I am proud of what I am doing. The part I like least is being away from my home and family so much. I have deployed twelve times since I've been in the Army.

Q: What personal qualities do you think are most important for a Green Beret?

A: First and foremost, you must be self-driven. You have to understand that you're responsible for getting things done and making yourself and your mission succeed. Another important quality is integrity. You have to do the right thing because of your integrity, because in Special Forces we have to trust each other and depend on each other. Another quality that's important is having a personality that allows you to make the best of any situation.

Q: What advice can you offer to high school students who may be interested in becoming Green Berets?

A: If you want this type of career, start preparing for it in high school. Don't get involved with drugs or criminal activities because you will not be able to join special forces if you have a criminal record. Focus on your education since special forces units want intelligent, well-educated people and you will have to take intelligence tests and knowledge tests when you apply. Maintain your health and physical fitness because these are also important. And remember, if you want this career, take responsibility for making it happen.

Find Out More

Naval Special Warfare/Naval Special Operations (NSW/NSO)
website: www.navy.com/careers/special-operations.html
This website contains detailed information about NSW/NSO missions, specialized units, training, and requirements.

Today's Military
website: http://todaysmilitary.com
This Department of Defense website has information about military branches, how to join, training, job descriptions, and benefits for those interested in learning about military careers.

US Air Force Special Operations Command (AFSOC)
website: www.afsoc.af.mil
The AFSOC website contains information about special forces missions, qualifications, and training.

US Army Special Operations Command (SOC)
website: www.soc.mil
The Army SOC website has detailed information about all army special operations units, including history, job descriptions, requirements, and training.

US Coast Guard Deployable Specialized Forces
website: www.uscg.mil/hq/cg5/cg532/pwcs.asp
This Coast Guard website contains information about the Coast Guard Deployable Specialized Forces teams, their history, and missions.

US Marine Corps Forces Special Operations Command
website: www.marsoc.marines.mil
This Marine Corps website has detailed information about its special operations units, missions, and qualifications.

US Special Operations Command (SOCOM)
website: www.socom.mil
SOCOM oversees all US special operations forces except those in the Coast Guard. Its website has information about SOCOM's role and about each military branch's special forces units.

Other Jobs in the Special Forces

Air Force Special Operations
Weather Team

Air Force Tactical Air Control
Party Specialists

Army Delta Force

Army Fourth Psychological
Operations Group

Army Ninety-Fifth Civil Affairs
Brigade

Army Seventy-Fifth Ranger
Regiment

Coast Guard Coastal Riverine
Squadron and Group

Coast Guard Maritime Security
Response Team

Coast Guard National Strike
Force

Coast Guard Port Security Unit

Coast Guard Regional Dive
Locker Diver

Coast Guard Tactical Law
Enforcement Team

Marine Corps Forces Special
Operations Command

Marine Corps Division
Reconnaissance

Marine Corps Radio
Reconnaissance Team

Marine Maritime Raid Force

Marine Raider Regiment

Marine Raider Support Group

Naval Special Warfare Aviation

Navy Aviation Rescue Swimmer

Navy Diver

Navy Explosive Ordnance
Disposal Squad

Editor's Note: The online *Occupational Outlook Handbook* of the US Department of Labor's Bureau of Labor Statistics is an excellent source of information on jobs in hundreds of career fields including many of those listed here. The *Occupational Outlook Handbook* may be accessed online at www.bls.gov/ooh/.

Index